Sports Illustrated KIDS

ULTIMATE COLLECTION OF PRO HOCKEY RECORDS 2015

BY SHANE FREDERICK

capstone
young readers

Sports Illustrated Kids Ultimate Collection of Pro Hockey Records 2015
is published by Capstone Young Readers,
1710 Roe Crest Drive, North Mankato, Minnesota 56003.
www.capstonepub.com

Library of Congress Cataloging-in-Publication Data
Cataloging-in-publication information is on file with the Library of Congress.

ISBN 978-1-4914-1962-5

Edited by Clare Lewis and Anthony Wacholtz
Designed by Richard Parker and Eric Manske
Media Research by Eric Gohl
Production by Helen McCreath

Photo Credits
123RF: Rocco Macri, 98; AP Images: The Canadian Press, 76, Paul Connors, 113t; Corbis:
Bettmann, 120t, Underwood & Underwood, 43b; Dreamstime: Jerry Coli, cover (right);
Getty Images: Bruce Bennett Studios, 21b, 29b, 73, 77b, 78b, 79t, 94b, 105t, 112, NHLI/Denis
Brodeur, 36t, 67b, NHLI/Steve Babineau, 22b, 34b, 69; Library of Congress: 124t; Newscom:
Ai Wire/Randy Wilson, 118b, Icon SMI/IHA, 42b, 95b, Icon SMI/John Cordes, 47, iPhoto Inc./
Dave Abel, 24, iPhoto Inc./Dennis Miles, 92t, KRT/Huy Nguyen, 117b, KRT/Roy Gallop, 15b,
Louis Deluca, 110b, MCT/Ralph Lauer, 111, UPI Photo Service/Bill Pugliano, 67t, UPI Photo
Service/Michael Bush, 23b; Shutterstock: Fahrner, 105b, Marty Ellis, 60–61 (background),
113b, Nip, 8–9, Rob Marmion, 10–11, Zeliksone Veronika, 62t; Sports Illustrated: Bob Martin,
102b, Bob Rosato, 25b, 26t, 40, 49t, 55bl, 79b, 95t, Damian Strohmeyer, 14b, 16–17, 25t, 35t,
37, 46, 49b, 57bl, 82, 121t, 121b, David E. Klutho, cover (left), 2m, 2b, 3, 4¬–5, 6, 9t, 9br, 11t,
13, 14t, 18, 19t, 20t, 21t, 22t, 23t, 27t, 33t, 36b, 42t, 43t, 44, 45b, 50b, 51t, 51bmr, 52b, 53ml,
53mr, 54r, 55bmr, 56t, 57bml, 57bmr, 57br, 60r, 61t, 61m, 62b, 63t, 64–65, 66, 70, 71, 78t, 80–81,
84t, 85b, 86b, 87b, 89, 90, 91t, 91b, 93t, 93b, 94t, 96t, 97, 99, 100t, 103t, 103b, 104l, 104r, 107t,
107b, 108t, 108b, 109t, 109m, 109b, 114–115, 120b, 123, 125, Heinz Kluetmeier, 77t, 85t, 102t,
Hy Peskin, 12, 48, 51bl, 51br, 55t, 63b, 86t, 92b, 100b, 119r, John D. Hanlon, 2t, 32, 33b, 52m,
59t, 101, John G. Zimmerman, 55br, 118t, John Iacono, 74t, 83b, 124b, Lane Stewart, 84b,
Manny Millan, 26b, 28, 31, 53r, 60l, 68b, 88, Richard Meek, 19b, 50t, 83t, Robert Beck, 7, 27b,
45t, 52t, 56b, 57t, 58b, 87t, 106, 110t, 116, Simon Bruty, 38–39, Tony Triolo, cover (middle),
15t, 20b, 29t, 30, 34t, 35b, 41, 51bml, 53l, 54l, 55bml, 58t, 59b, 61b, 68t, 74b, 117t, 119l, Walter
Iooss Jr., 75, Wikimedia: Kendrick Erickson, 96b, spcbrass, 72

Design Elements
Shutterstock: ArtyFree, B Calkins, Dusty Cline, fmua, ssuaphotos

Printed in Canada.
092014   007105

TABLE OF CONTENTS

INTRODUCTION

It's easy to see why enthusiasm surrounds hockey. The sport has speed and skill, hard hits, and intensity. Game-winning goals are celebrated with group hugs, and even the fiercest rivals line up and shake hands after a grueling playoff series. Each game opens the possibility for an amazing goal or a shocking check into the boards.

The game of hockey has been fiercely competitive ever since 1892, for it was then that Lord Frederick Arthur Stanley, Governor General of Canada, donated a trophy for the purposes of deciding the best hockey team in the land. The Stanley Cup, as it came to be known, was subsequently highly sought after by the best players and teams. It is still awarded

each season to the top team in the National Hockey League (NHL).

Another way to decide the best of the best through the ages is by keeping records. Setting a record is a big deal. It's a historic event. A record establishes a player or team as one of the greats in contrast to others and is used as a measuring stick for young and future players.

Hockey today is as colorful, competitive, and exciting as it's ever been. The pages that follow represent the finest players, teams, and feats that the dazzling sport of hockey has ever seen.

LET'S PLAY HOCKEY

The play begins with a bone-crushing hit. The defenseman drives the opposing puck carrier into the boards, rattling the glass. He scoops up the puck as his victim falls to the ice. The defenseman passes it ahead to a forward flying through the neutral zone. The forward catches the puck and makes a fancy move to get around a defender. He fakes a shot during the breakaway to get the goalie moving. He follows the fake with a rocket shot that sends the puck over the goalie's shoulder and into the net. Goal!

A big hit, a beautiful pass, a crazy deke, and a goal. It's the perfect combination to send any crowd into a frenzy, whether it's at a city rink, a high school arena, or a 20,000-seat NHL stadium.

THE EVOLUTION OF HOCKEY

The game of hockey that we know today looked much different in the 1800s, when the sport was invented. Long before there were pro teams in southern California, Texas, and Florida—and even a few years before the game moved indoors—the rules were much different than they are now.

The object of hockey was the same: Score goals by shooting a small, flat puck into your opponent's net while trying to stop the opposing team from doing the same. But in the late 1800s, it was not the high-flying, hard-hitting, wide-open game we watch today. Back then players were not allowed to pass the puck forward. Lifting the puck off the ice while taking a shot on goal was illegal too.

But hockey is an ever-evolving game. The rules have been tweaked since the first player got slashed across the wrists. Eventually the game opened up, and players were allowed to pass the puck forward. First they could make such a pass only within one of the three zones. Later they were able to pass from the defensive zone to the neutral zone. The only offside rule remaining is when an attacking player crosses the blue line and into the offensive zone before the puck.

The rule about not lifting the puck when trying to shoot a goal was dismissed too. That's why goalies started wearing big pads, giant gloves, and facemasks.

THE RINK

The game of hockey was first played on the frozen lakes and ponds of Canada and the northern United States. When it comes to the NHL, the game is played in arenas and stadiums that hold as many as 20,000 fans. In most cases, the ice surface is 200 feet (61 meters) long and 85 feet (26 m) wide. Boards about 4 feet (1.2 m) high surround the ice to keep the puck in play. Safety glass is placed on top of the boards to protect the spectators from pucks. The rink is divided into three zones, two offensive/defensive zones and the neutral zone.

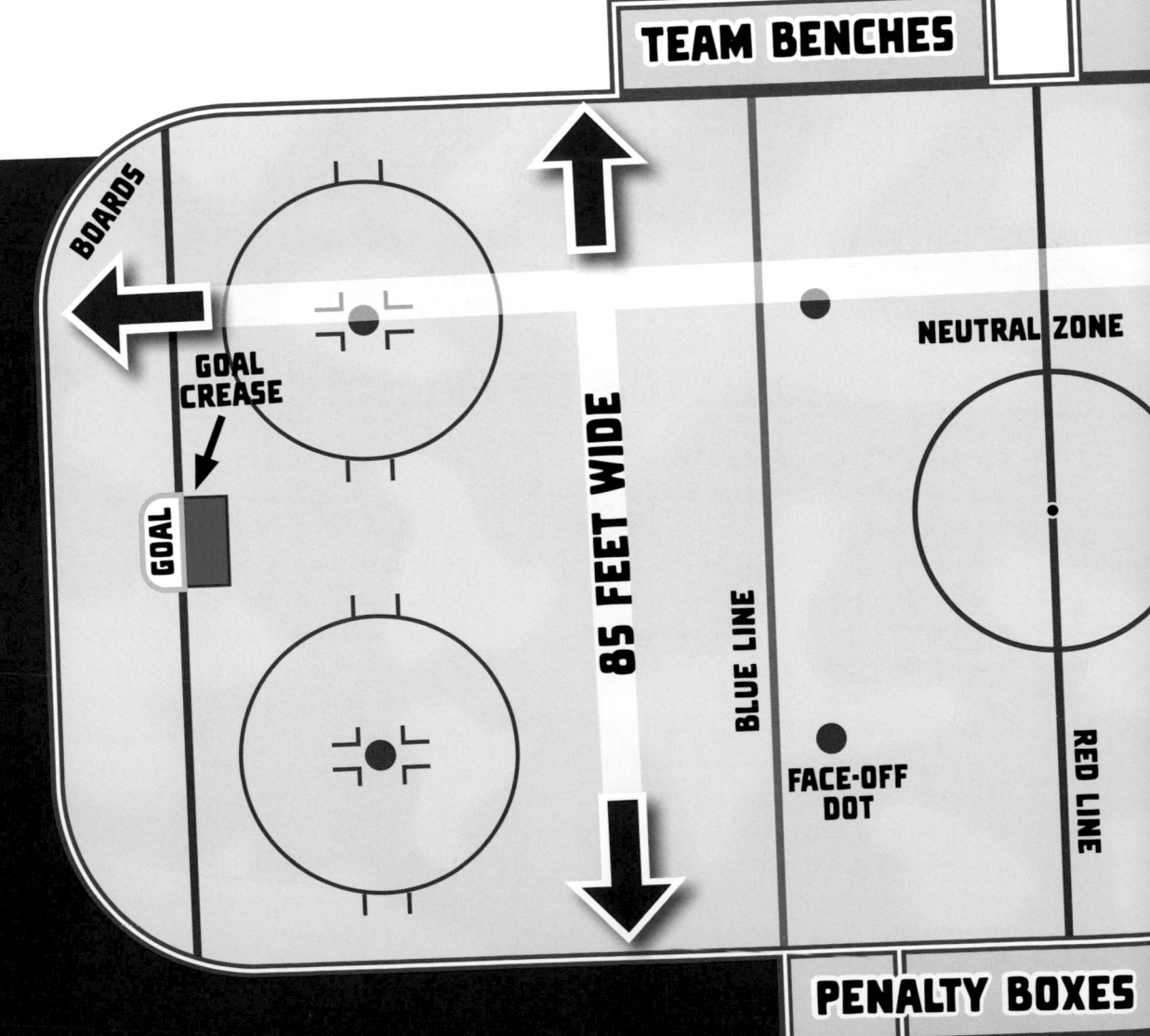

TEAM BENCHES

BOARDS

GOAL CREASE

GOAL

85 FEET WIDE

NEUTRAL ZONE

BLUE LINE

FACE-OFF DOT

RED LINE

PENALTY BOXES

OTHER RINKS

International hockey, such as in the Olympics, is played on ice surfaces larger than NHL rinks. Olympic ice is 200 feet (61 m) long and 100 feet (30 m) wide. Many college teams in the United States also play on international-sized ice. The extra space on the rink often favors the game's better skaters.

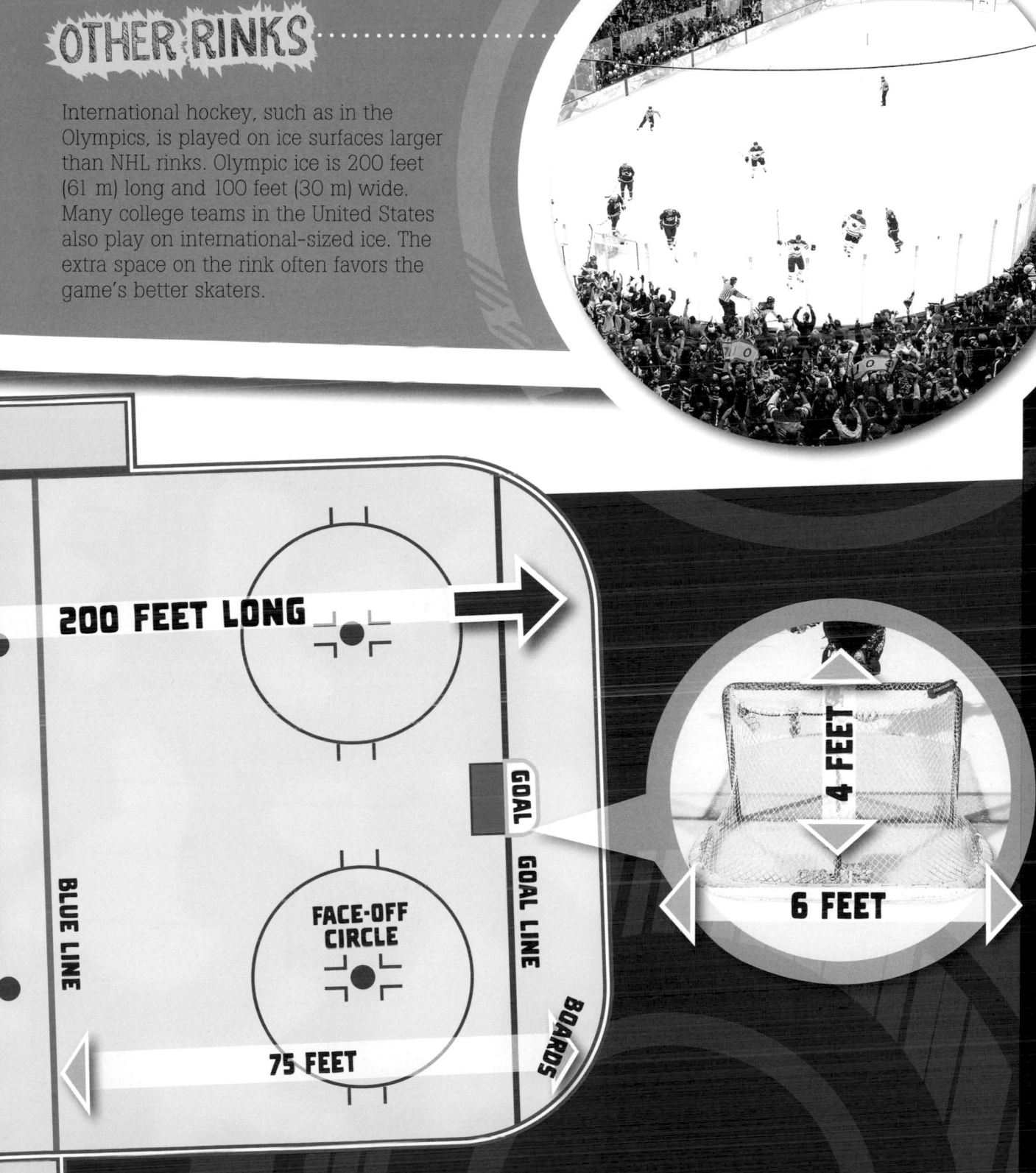

200 FEET LONG

BLUE LINE

FACE-OFF CIRCLE

75 FEET

GOAL

GOAL LINE

BOARDS

4 FEET

6 FEET

POSITIONS

When teams are playing at full strength, each team has six players on the ice: three forwards (center, left wing, right wing), two defensemen, and a goaltender.

TRIVIA

Name that Position!
Can you match the position of each of the hockey players?

1.

2.

2.

3.

4.

5.

POSITIONS
CENTER
LEFT WING
RIGHT WING
DEFENSEMAN
GOALTENDER

PENALTY PUNISHMENT

A player who commits a serious penalty, such as trying to injure another player, is immediately ejected from the game. When players are called for other penalties, such as hooking, charging, or slashing, they must leave the rink and sit in the penalty box for two, four, or five minutes. While they are in the box, their teammates must play short-handed. The short-handed team may have three or four skaters and a goalie on the ice while the other team is on the power play. Teams play short-handed until the penalty time ends or until the opponent scores a goal. Sometimes players on opposite teams get called for penalties at about the same time. Then the teams each play with four skaters and a goalie. Teams put a lot of practice into their power play and short-handed units, which are called special teams.

5. _____ 2. _____

4. _____

3. _____ 2. _____

1. _____

FACT:

If a team is down by a goal with only a few minutes remaining in the game, the coach may decide to pull the goalie off the ice. In the goalie's place, the coach can add another skater. Although it leaves the net wide open, it gives the team a 6-on-5 advantage and a better chance to score a goal.

Answer: 1. goaltender 2. defenseman 3. left wing 4. center 5. right wing

EQUIPMENT

When hockey was first played in the late 1800s, players only used a pair of skates and a stick. Over time protective gear was added, including padding and hard plastic for shins, knees, shoulders, and elbows. It took awhile for players, especially at the professional level, to get used to wearing helmets and masks.

The first NHL goalie to wear a mask was Jacques Plante. After getting his face bloodied by a puck in a 1959 game, Plante got stitched up and returned to the game with a mask. He continued to wear a mask, even though his coach didn't approve. Then more goalies started wearing masks. Andy Brown of the Pittsburgh Penguins was the last goalie to play in a game without a mask, in 1974.

In 1979 the NHL required all of the draft picks from that year forward to wear helmets. The league allowed players already in the league to play without headgear. One of the players, 1978 draft pick Craig MacTavish, played without a helmet until he retired in 1997—18 years after the helmet rule was first enforced.

In 2013 the NHL required new players to wear plastic visors for eye protection. Younger players often wear full face shields or metal cages.

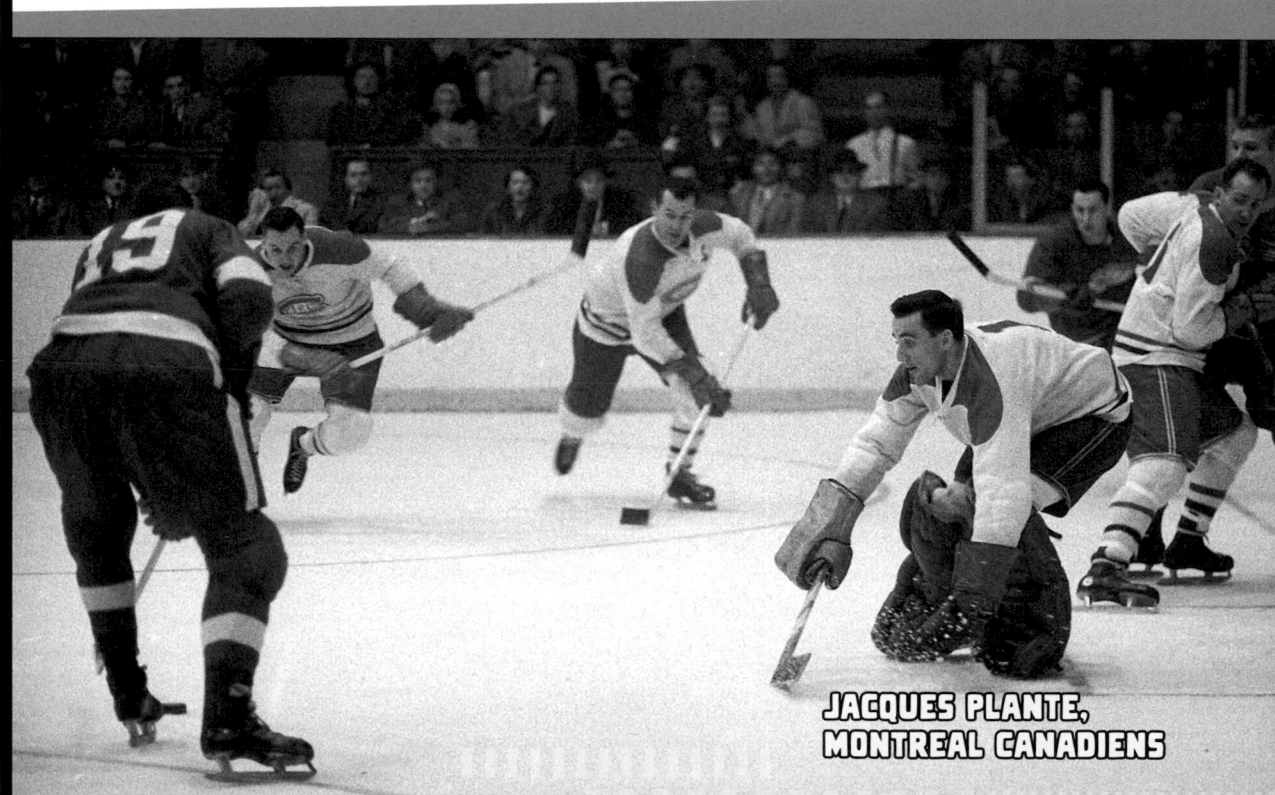

JACQUES PLANTE, MONTREAL CANADIENS

HELMET

EYE SHIELD

MOUTHGUARD

SHOULDER PADS

JERSEY

ELBOW PADS

HOCKEY PANTS
(BREEZERS)

GLOVES

SHIN PADS

SKATES

STICKS **ALL AROUND**

Players pass and shoot the puck with hockey sticks.
The sticks come in various lengths and are chosen
according to the player's size. They have a curved
blade at the bottom to control the puck. In the early
days hockey sticks were made of wood and had a
flat blade. Today most sticks are made of high-tech,
composite materials that make them lighter and
stronger. Some of the top players can use the sticks
to fire shots that go more than 100 mph.

STICK

UNIFORMS

Football has helmets and baseball has caps, but hockey teams are defined by their jerseys. The New York Rangers have been known as the Blueshirts since their early days. The St. Louis Blues are nicknamed the "Blue Notes" because of the big, blue-winged musical note that graces the front of their jerseys.

DRESSED FOR SUCCESS

So what are the best uniforms in the NHL? Ask 30 fans and you might get 30 different answers. Here are a few that have gotten rave reviews over the years—as well as a couple that have caused critics to hold their noses. The Penguins, like Pittsburgh's other professional sports teams, wear black, yellow, and white. But originally they wore light blue sweaters. In recent years the team has occasionally brought back the powder blues. One of those times was for the Winter Classic, a pro game played in an outdoor arena.

THE GOOD

The Montreal Canadiens are one of the NHL's original teams. The team has worn similar red, white, and blue jerseys since the league started in 1917. Their "CH" logo is instantly recognizable. It stands for the team's official French name, Le Club de Hockey Canadien. (French is the official language of the Canadian province of Quebec.)

Many NHL jerseys feature several colors, but not the Detroit Red Wings' jerseys. They keep it simple and classy with red and white. The jerseys have one of the sport's most unique logos—the winged wheel—across the chest. Other teams have followed the Wings with their own feathered logos, including the Blues and the Flyers.

THE UGLY

Critics cried foul when the New York Islanders tried to change the jerseys that won four straight Stanley Cups. The logo featured a salty fisherman who looked like the character on a box of frozen seafood. When the Isles skated onto the ice to play their rivals—the New York Rangers—opposing fans repeatedly chanted, "We want fish sticks!" The Islanders returned to their classic jerseys in 1984 after one season.

THE BAD

It has taken years for the Vancouver Canucks to perfect their uniforms. While their current blue, green, and white sweaters end up on best-of lists, earlier sweaters were hard on the eyes. With black, orange, and yellow as their official colors, the Canucks once sported a giant V that stretched from the player's shoulders to his belly button.

KEEPING WARM

Do you know why hockey jerseys are sometimes called sweaters? The first hockey teams wore warm, wool, knitted sweaters when they played on outdoor ice rinks in the middle of cold winters. As games moved into indoor rinks, players wanted jerseys made out of lighter materials.

CHAPTER 2

SKATER RECORDS

Wayne Gretzky doesn't own all of the NHL's individual records. It just seems that way. "The Great One" not only broke Gordie Howe's goal-scoring record. He also shattered his hero's points mark, finishing his career with 2,857 goals and assists combined. In fact, if you took away Gretzky's goals, his career assist total would still be enough to be the NHL's all-time points leader!

It seems likely that Gretzky's points record will never be broken. Mark Messier, Gretzky's former Edmonton Oilers teammate, has come closest. Messier finished his career with 1,887 points, but that's almost 1,000 points less than Gretzky.

When it comes to individual players, records can define their greatness, whether it's over a career, a season, or even one game.

If Gretzky's scoring records won't fall, what will? Perhaps it will be Jaromir Jagr's game-winning goals record of 124. What about Ray Bourque's record for goals by a defenseman? Or Tim Kerr's single-season record for power-play goals?

▼ **Wayne Gretzky**

SCORING

⬤ POINTS

CARERR

1.	Wayne Gretzky	2,857	Oilers/Kings/Blues/Rangers	1979–1999
2.	Mark Messier	1,887	Oilers/Rangers/Canucks	1979–2004
3.	Gordie Howe	1,850	Red Wings/Whalers	1946–1971, 1979–1980
4.	Ron Francis	1,798	Whalers/Pens/Hurricanes/Maple Leafs	1981–2004
5.	Marcel Dionne	1,771	Red Wings/Kings/Rangers	1971–1989
6.	Steve Yzerman	1,755	Red Wings	1983–2006
7.	Jaromir Jagr	1,755	Penguins/Capitals/Rangers/Flyers/Stars/Bruins/Devils	1990–2004, 2005–2008, 2011–2014*
8.	Mario Lemieux	1,723	Penguins	1984–1994, 1995–1997, 2000–2006
9.	Joe Sakic	1,641	Nordiques/Avalanche	1988–2009
10.	Phil Esposito	1,590	Blackhawks/Bruins/Rangers	1963–1981

*Active player

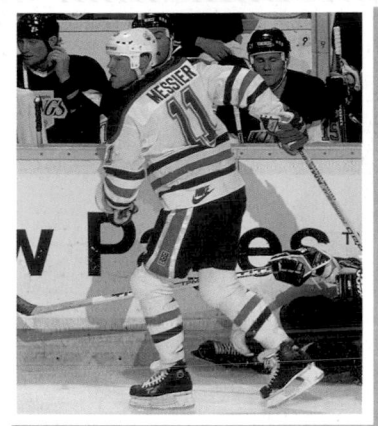
▼ Mark Messier

▼ Gordie Howe

WORLD HOCKEY ASSOCIATION

Wayne Gretzky also scored 110 points (46 goals, 64 assists) in the World Hockey Association. He played one year in the WHA before the Oilers merged into the NHL. Gordie Howe played six seasons in the WHA after a long career with the Red Wings and scored 508 points (174 goals, 334 assists) in that league.

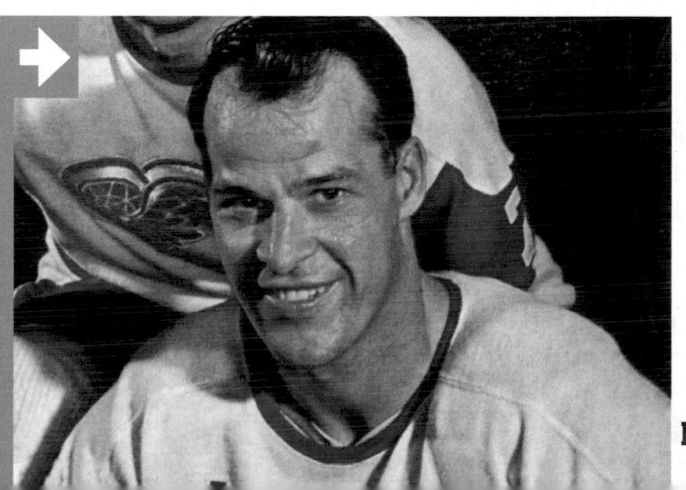

 # POINTS

SINGLE SEASON

1.	Wayne Gretzky	215	Oilers	1985–86
2.	Wayne Gretzky	212	Oilers	1981–82
3.	Wayne Gretzky	208	Oilers	1984–85
4.	Wayne Gretzky	205	Oilers	1983–84
5.	Mario Lemieux	199	Penguins	1988–89
6.	Wayne Gretzky	196	Oilers	1982–83
7.	Wayne Gretzky	183	Oilers	1986–87
8.	Mario Lemieux	168	Penguins	1987–88
	Wayne Gretzky	168	Kings	1988–89
10.	Wayne Gretzky	164	Oilers	1980–81

▼ Bryan Trottier

POINTS ALL AROUND

Darryl Sittler of the Toronto Maple Leafs compiled 10 points in a single game in 1976. He scored six goals and assisted on four others in an 11-4 victory over the Boston Bruins. On 16 occasions players have recorded eight-point games. Mario Lemieux did it three times, and Wayne Gretzky did it twice. The record for points in a period is six, set by the New York Islanders' Bryan Trottier in 1978.

RECORD FACT Joe Malone scored seven goals in a game in 1920 for the Quebec Bulldogs. Seven players have scored six goals in a game, including Malone that same season. Eleven players have scored four goals in one period of play.

 **GOALS**

CAREER ||||||||||||||||||||||||||||||||||||||||

1.	Wayne Gretzky	894	Oilers/Kings/Blues/ Rangers	1979–1999
2.	Gordie Howe	801	Red Wings/Whalers	1946–1971, 1979–1980
3.	Brett Hull	741	Flames/Blues/Stars/ Red Wings/Coyotes	1986–2006
4.	Marcel Dionne	731	Red Wings/Kings/ Rangers	1971–1989
5.	Phil Esposito	717	Blackhawks/Bruins/ Rangers	1963–1981
6.	Mike Gartner	708	Capitals/North Stars/ Rangers/Maple Leafs/ Coyotes	1979–1998
7.	Jaromir Jagr	681	Penguins/Capitals/ Rangers/Flyers/Stars/ Bruins/ Devils	1990–2004, 2005–2008, 2011–2014*
8.	Mark Messier	694	Oilers/Rangers/ Canucks	1979–2004
9.	Steve Yzerman	692	Red Wings	1983–2006
10.	Mario Lemieux	690	Penguins	1984–1994, 1995–1997, 2000–2006

*Active player

SINGLE SEASON ||||||||||||||||||||||||||||||||||||

1.	Wayne Gretzky	92	Oilers	1981–82
2.	Wayne Gretzky	87	Oilers	1983–84
3.	Brett Hull	86	Blues	1990–91
4.	Mario Lemieux	85	Penguins	1988–89
5.	Phil Esposito	76	Bruins	1970–71
	Alexander Mogilny	76	Sabres	1992–93
	Teemu Selanne	76	Jets	1992–93
8.	Wayne Gretzky	73	Oilers	1984–85
9.	Brett Hull	72	Blues	1989–90
10.	Wayne Gretzky	71	Oilers	1982–83
	Jari Kurri	71	Oilers	1984–85

▲ Alexander Mogilny

POWER-PLAY GOALS

CAREER ||||||||||||||||||||||||||||||||||||||||||

1.	Dave Andreychuk	274	Sabres/Maple Leafs/ Devils/Bruins/ Avalanche/Lightning	1982–2006
2.	Brett Hull	265	Flames/Blues/Stars/ Red Wings/Coyotes	1986–2006
3.	Teemu Selanne	255	Jets/Ducks/Sharks/ Avalanche	1992–2014
4.	Phil Esposito	249	Blackhawks/Bruins/ Rangers	1963–1981
5.	Luc Robitaille	247	Kings/Penguins/ Rangers/Red Wings	1986–2006
6.	Brendan Shanahan	237	Devils/Blues/Whalers/ Red Wings/Rangers	1987–2009
7.	Mario Lemieux	236	Penguins	1984–1994, 1995–1997, 2000–2006
8.	Marcel Dionne	234	Red Wings/Kings/ Rangers	1971–1989
9.	Dino Ciccarelli	232	North Stars/ Capitals/Red Wings/ Lightning/Panthers	1980–1999
10.	Mike Gartner	217	Capitals/North Stars/ Rangers/Maple Leafs/Coyotes	1979–1998

SINGLE SEASON ||||||||||||||||||||||||||||||||

1.	Tim Kerr	34	Flyers	1985–86
2.	Dave Andreychuk	32	Sabres/ Maple Leafs	1992–93
3.	Mario Lemieux	31	Penguins	1988–89
	Mario Lemieux	31	Penguins	1995–96
	Joe Nieuwendyk	31	Flames	1987–88
6.	Michel Goulet	29	Nordiques	1987–88
	Brett Hull	29	Blues	1990–91
	Brett Hull	29	Blues	1992–93
9.	Four players tied with	28		

▲ Tim Kerr

SHORT-HANDED GOALS

▼ Steve Yzerman

CAREER

#	Player		Teams	Years
1.	Wayne Gretzky	73	Oilers/Kings/Blues/Rangers	1979–1999
2.	Mark Messier	63	Oilers/Rangers/Canucks	1979–2004
3.	Steve Yzerman	50	Red Wings	1983–2006
4.	Mario Lemieux	49	Penguins	1984–1994, 1995–1997, 2000–2006
5.	Butch Goring	40	Kings/Islanders/Bruins	1969–1985
6.	Dave Poulin	39	Flyers/Bruins/Capitals	1982–1995
7.	Jari Kurri	37	Oilers/Kings/Rangers/Ducks/Avalanche	1980–1990, 1991–1998
8.	Sergei Fedorov	36	Red Wings/Ducks/Blue Jackets/Capitals	1990–2009
9.	Theoren Fleury	35	Flames/Avalanche/Rangers/Blackhawks	1988–2003
	Dirk Graham	35	North Stars/Blackhawks	1983–1995

SHORT-HANDED GOALS

A team is short-handed when one of its players is in the penalty box and the other team is on a power play. Despite having fewer players, the short-handed team still has the opportunity to score. Theoren Fleury of the Calgary Flames holds the record for short-handed goals in a single game. He scored three goals on the opponents' power plays in a game in 1991.

▼ Theoren Fleury

SHORT-HANDED GOALS

SINGLE SEASON

1.	Mario Lemieux	13	Penguins	1988–89
2.	Wayne Gretzky	12	Oilers	1983–84
3.	Wayne Gretzky	11	Oilers	1984–85
4.	Marcel Dionne	10	Red Wings	1974–75
	Dirk Graham	10	Blackhawks	1988–89
	Mario Lemieux	10	Penguins	1987–88
7.	Paul Coffey	9	Oilers	1985–86
	Kent Nilsson	9	Flames	1983–84
	Brian Rolston	9	Bruins	2001–02
10.	Many players tied with	8		

OVERTIME GOALS

CAREER

1.	Jaromir Jagr	18	Penguins/Capitals/Rangers/Flyers/Stars/Bruins/Devils	1990–2004, 2005–2008, 2011–2014*
2.	Patrik Elias	16	Devils	1995–2014*
3.	Sergei Fedorov	15	Red Wings/Ducks/Blue Jackets/Capitals	1990–2009
	Mats Sundin	15	Nordiques/Maple Leafs/Canucks	1990–2009
	Alex Ovechkin	15	Capitals	2005–2014*
6.	Ilya Kovalchuk	14	Thrashers/Devils	2001–2013
7.	Scott Niedermayer	13	Devils/Ducks	1991–2010
	Olli Jokinen	13	Kings/Islanders/Panthers/Coyotes/Flames/Rangers/Jets	1997–2014*
9.	Brett Hull	12	Flames/Blues/Stars/Red Wings/Coyotes	1986-2006
	Brendan Shanahan	12	Devils/Blues/Whalers/Red Wings/Rangers	1987–2009

*Active player

RECORD FACT Joe Malone of the Montreal Canadiens scored 44 goals in 20 games in 1917–18. He holds the record for the best season average of 2.2 goals per game. Wayne Gretzky holds the NHL record for points per game for a season. In 1983–84 he had 205 points in 74 games, a 2.77 average.

GAME-WINNING GOALS

CAREER ||||||||||||||||||||||||||||||||||||||||

1.	Jaromir Jagr	124	Penguins/Capitals/Rangers/Flyers/Stars/Bruins/Devils	1990–2004, 2005–2008, 2011–2014*
2.	Phil Esposito	118	Blackhawks/Bruins/Rangers	1963–1981
3.	Brett Hull	110	Flames/Blues/Stars/Red Wings/Coyotes	1986–2006
	Teemu Selanne	110	Jets/Ducks/Sharks/Avalanche	1992–2014*
5.	Brendan Shanahan	109	Devils/Blues/Whalers/Red Wings/Rangers	1987–2009
6.	Guy Lafleur	97	Canadiens/Rangers/Nordiques	1971–1985, 1988–1991
7.	Mats Sundin	96	Nordiques/Maple Leafs/Canucks	1990–2009
8.	Steve Yzerman	94	Red Wings	1983–2006
9.	Sergei Fedorov	93	Red Wings/Ducks/Blue Jackets/Capitals	1990–2009
	Joe Nieuwendyk	93	Flames/Stars/Devils/Maple Leafs/Panthers	1986–2007

*Active player

SINGLE SEASON ||||||||||||||||||||||||||||||||||||

1.	Phil Esposito	16	Bruins	1970–71
	Phil Esposito	16	Bruins	1971–72
	Michel Goulet	16	Nordiques	1983–84
4.	Pavel Bure	14	Panthers	1999–00
5.	Peter Bondra	13	Capitals	1997–98
	Jari Kurri	13	Oilers	1984–85
	Cam Neely	13	Bruins	1993–94
	Jeremy Roenick	13	Blackhawks	1991–92
9.	Many players tied with	12		

▲ Pavel Bure

PENALTY SHOT GOALS

CAREER

1.	Pavel Bure	7	Canucks/Panthers/Rangers	1991–2003
2.	Mario Lemieux	6	Penguins	1984–1994, 1995–1997, 2000–2006
3.	Vincent Lecavalier	5	Lightning	1998–2014*
4.	Joe Sakic	4	Nordiques/Avalanche	1988–2009
	Mats Sundin	4	Nordiques/Maple Leafs/Canucks	1990–2009
	David Vyborny	4	Blue Jackets	2000–2008

*Active player

HAT TRICKS

CAREER

1.	Wayne Gretzky	50	Oilers/Kings/Blues/Rangers	1979–1999
2.	Mario Lemieux	40	Penguins	1984–1994 1995–1997, 2000–2006
3.	Mike Bossy	39	Islanders	1977–1987
4.	Brett Hull	33	Flames/Blues/Stars/Red Wings/Coyotes	1986–2006
5.	Phil Esposito	32	Blackhawks/Bruins/Rangers	1963–1981
6.	Marcel Dionne	28	Red Wings/Kings/Rangers	1971–1989
	Bobby Hull	28	Blackhawks/Jets/Whalers	1957–1980
8.	Maurice Richard	26	Canadiens	1942–1960
9.	Cy Denneny	25	Senators/Bruins	1917–1929
10.	Jari Kurri	23	Oilers/Kings/Rangers/Ducks/Avalanche	1980–1990, 1991–1998

A player can earn a hat trick by scoring three goals in a single game. Wayne Gretzky has the single-season record for hat tricks in a season with 10. In fact, he racked up 10 hat tricks in a season twice! Mario Lemieux and Mike Bossy each had a nine-hat-trick season.

POINTS IN A ROOKIE SEASON

▼ Sidney Crosby

ROOKIE SEASON				
1.	Teemu Selanne	132	Jets	1992–93
2.	Peter Stastny	109	Nordiques	1980–81
3.	Alex Ovechkin	106	Capitals	2005–06
4.	Dale Hawerchuk	103	Jets	1981–82
5.	Sidney Crosby	102	Penguins	2005–06
	Joe Juneau	102	Bruins	1992–93
7.	Mario Lemieux	100	Penguins	1984–85
8.	Neal Broten	98	North Stars	1981–82
9.	Bryan Trottier	95	Islanders	1975–76
10.	Joe Nieuwendyk	92	Flames	1987–88
	Barry Pederson	92	Bruins	1981–82

GOALS IN A ROOKIE SEASON

ROOKIE SEASON				
1.	Teemu Selanne	76	Jets	1992–93
2.	Mike Bossy	53	Islanders	1977–78
3.	Alex Ovechkin	52	Capitals	2005–06
4.	Joe Nieuwendyk	51	Flames	1987–88
5.	Dale Hawerchuk	45	Jets	1981–82
	Luc Robitaille	45	Kings	1986–87
7.	Rick Martin	44	Sabres	1971–72
	Barry Pederson	44	Bruins	1981–82
9.	Steve Larmer	43	Blackhawks	1982–83
	Mario Lemieux	43	Penguins	1984–85

▲ Alex Ovechkin

 **ASSISTS**

CAREER

1.	Wayne Gretzky	1,963	Oilers/Kings/Blues/Rangers	1979–1999
2.	Ron Francis	1,249	Whalers/Penguins/Hurricanes/Maple Leafs	1981–2004
3.	Mark Messier	1,193	Oilers/Rangers/Canucks	1979–2004
4.	Ray Bourque	1,169	Bruins/Avalanche	1979–2001
5.	Paul Coffey	1,135	Oilers/Penguins/Kings/Red Wings/Whalers/Flyers/Blackhawks/Hurricanes/Bruins	1980–2001
6.	Adam Oates	1,079	Red Wings/Blues/Bruins/Capitals/Flyers/Ducks/Oilers	1985–2004
7.	Steve Yzerman	1,063	Red Wings	1983–2006
8.	Jaromir Jagr	1,050	Penguins/Capitals/Rangers/Flyers/Stars/Bruins/Devils	1990–2004 2005–2008 2011–2014
9.	Gordie Howe	1,049	Red Wings/Whalers	1946–1971, 1979–1980
10.	Marcel Dionne	1,040	Red Wings/Kings/Rangers	1971–1989

RECORD FACT Goal scorers don't get all of the glory. Each time a puck goes into the net, official scorers can award up to two assists to the passers who set up the goal. When it comes to the scoring charts, an assist is worth one point, the same as a goal.

⬤ ASSISTS

SINGLE SEASON

1.	Wayne Gretzky	163	Oilers	1985–86
2.	Wayne Gretzky	135	Oilers	1984–85
3.	Wayne Gretzky	125	Oilers	1982–83
4.	Wayne Gretzky	122	Kings	1990–91
5.	Wayne Gretzky	121	Oilers	1986–87
6.	Wayne Gretzky	120	Oilers	1981–82
7.	Wayne Gretzky	118	Oilers	1983–84
8.	Wayne Gretzky	114	Kings	1988–89
	Mario Lemieux	114	Penguins	1988–89
10.	Wayne Gretzky	109	Oilers	1987–88
	Wayne Gretzky	109	Oilers	1980–81

ASSIST MANIA

▼ Dale Hawerchuk

Wayne Gretzky holds the record for most assists in one game. Three times in his career with Edmonton—in 1980, 1985, and 1986—he assisted on seven goals in a game. The only other player to have seven assists in a game was Billy Taylor of the Detroit Red Wings in 1947. The record for most assists in a single period is five set by the Winnipeg Jets' Dale Hawerchuk in 1984.

RECORD FACT Mark Messier assisted on more overtime goals than any other player, helping out on 18 over his career. Messier also scored eight overtime winners, giving him a record 26 overtime points for his 25 seasons.

POINTS BY A DEFENSEMAN

CAREER

1.	Ray Bourque	1,579	Bruins/Avalanche	1979–2001
2.	Paul Coffey	1,531	Oilers/Penguins/Kings/Red Wings/ Whalers/Flyers/Blackhawks/ Hurricanes/Bruins	1980–2001
3.	Al MacInnis	1,274	Flames/Blues	1981–2004
4.	Phil Housley	1,232	Sabres/Jets/Blues/Flames/Devils/ Capitals/Blackhawks/Maple Leafs	1982–2003
5.	Larry Murphy	1,216	Kings/Capitals/North Stars/Penguins/ Maple Leafs/ Red Wings	1980–2001
6.	Nicklas Lidstrom	1,142	Red Wings	1991–2012
7.	Denis Potvin	1,052	Islanders	1973–1988
8.	Brian Leetch	1,028	Rangers/Maple Leafs/Bruins	1987–2006
9.	Larry Robinson	958	Canadiens/Kings	1972–1992
10.	Chris Chelios	948	Canadiens/Blackhawks/ Red Wings/Thrashers	1983–2010

SINGLE SEASON

1.	Bobby Orr	139	Bruins	1970–71
2.	Paul Coffey	138	Oilers	1985–86
3.	Bobby Orr	135	Bruins	1974–75
4.	Paul Coffey	126	Oilers	1983–84
5.	Bobby Orr	122	Bruins	1973–74
6.	Paul Coffey	121	Oilers	1984–85
7.	Bobby Orr	120	Bruins	1969–70
8.	Bobby Orr	117	Bruins	1971–72
9.	Paul Coffey	113	Penguins	1988–89
10.	Paul Coffey	103	Penguins	1989–90
	Al MacInnis	103	Flames	1990–91

▲ **Raymond Bourque**

RECORD FACT Defenseman Ray Bourque holds the record for the most shots on goal for a career. During his 21 seasons, the Boston Bruins star put 6,206 shots on net.

GOALS BY A DEFENSEMAN

CAREER

1.	Ray Bourque	410	Bruins/Avalanche	1979–2001
2.	Paul Coffey	396	Oilers/Penguins/Kings/Red Wings/ Whalers/Flyers/Blackhawks/ Hurricanes/Bruins	1980–2001
3.	Al MacInnis	340	Flames/Blues	1981–2004
4.	Phil Housley	338	Sabres/Jets/Blues/Flames/Devils/ Capitals/Blackhawks/Maple Leafs	1982–2003
5.	Denis Potvin	310	Islanders	1973–1988
6.	Larry Murphy	287	Kings/Capitals/North Stars/Penguins/ Maple Leafs/ Red Wings	1980–2001
7.	Red Kelly	281	Red Wings/Maple Leafs	1947–1967
8.	Bobby Orr	270	Bruins/Blackhawks	1966–1979
9.	Nicklas Lidstrom	264	Red Wings	1991–2012
10.	Brian Leetch	247	Rangers/Maple Leafs/Bruins	1987–2006

SINGLE SEASON

1.	Paul Coffey	48	Oilers	1985–86
2.	Bobby Orr	46	Bruins	1974–75
3.	Paul Coffey	40	Oilers	1983–84
4.	Doug Wilson	39	Blackhawks	1981–82
5.	Paul Coffey	37	Oilers	1984–85
	Bobby Orr	37	Bruins	1970–71
	Bobby Orr	37	Bruins	1971–72
8.	Kevin Hatcher	34	Capitals	1992–93
9.	Bobby Orr	33	Bruins	1969–70
10.	Bobby Orr	32	Bruins	1973–74

▲ Denis Potvin

RECORD FACT Ian Turnbull of the Toronto Maple Leafs is the only defenseman in NHL history to score five goals in a game. He accomplished the feat in 1977. Eight defensemen have had four-goal games, including Turnbull in 1981.

ASSISTS BY A DEFENSEMAN

CAREER

1.	Ray Bourque	1,169	Bruins/Avalanche	1979–2001
2.	Paul Coffey	1,135	Oilers/Penguins/Kings/Red Wings/ Whalers/Flyers/Blackhawks/Hurricanes/ Bruins	1980–2001
3.	Al MacInnis	934	Flames/Blues	1981–2004
4.	Larry Murphy	929	Kings/Capitals/North Stars/Penguins/ Maple Leafs/ Red Wings	1980–2001
5.	Phil Housley	894	Sabres/Jets/Blues/Flames/Devils/ Capitals/Blackhawks/Maple Leafs	1982–2003
6.	Nicklas Lidstrom	878	Red Wings	1991–2012
7.	Brian Leetch	781	Rangers/Maple Leafs/Bruins	1987–2006
8.	Chris Chelios	763	Canadiens/Blackhawks/Red Wings/ Thrashers	1983–2010
9.	Larry Robinson	750	Canadiens/Kings	1972–1992
10.	Denis Potvin	742	Islanders	1973–1988

SINGLE SEASON

1.	Bobby Orr	102	Bruins	1970–71
2.	Paul Coffey	90	Oilers	1985–86
	Bobby Orr	90	Bruins	1973–74
4.	Bobby Orr	89	Bruins	1974–75
5.	Bobby Orr	87	Bruins	1969–70
6.	Paul Coffey	86	Oilers	1983–84
7.	Paul Coffey	84	Oilers	1984–85
8.	Paul Coffey	83	Penguins	1988–89
9.	Brian Leetch	80	Rangers	1991–92
	Bobby Orr	80	Bruins	1971–72

▲ Bobby Orr

RECORD FACT Six defensemen have six assists in a game. The list includes hockey legends Bobby Orr and Paul Coffey. The other four players are Babe Pratt, Pat Stapleton, Ron Stackhouse, and Gary Suter.

PLUS/MINUS

A player's plus/minus record shows how the team performed while the player was on the ice. The player earns a point if his team scores a goal at even strength or short-handed, and he loses a point if the other team scores a goal. However, power play goals and penalty shots are not included in the calculation. So, for example, a player is on the ice when his team scores a regular goal (+1) and a power play goal (no change), but the other team scores two goals (-2). The player's plus/minus would be -1.

▲ Patrice Bergeron led the NHL with a +36 during the 2011–12 season.

PLUS/MINUS

CAREER

1.	Larry Robinson	+730	Canadiens/Kings	1972–1992
2.	Bobby Orr	+597	Bruins/Blackhawks	1966–1979
3.	Ray Bourque	+528	Bruins/Avalanche	1979–2001
4.	Wayne Gretzky	+518	Oilers/Kings/Blues/Rangers	1979–1999
5.	Bobby Clarke	+506	Flyers	1969–1984
6.	Denis Potvin	+460	Islanders	1973–1988
	Serge Savard	+460	Canadiens/Jets	1966–1983
8.	Guy Lafleur	+453	Canadiens/Rangers/Nordiques	1971–1985, 1988–1991
9.	Bryan Trottier	+452	Islanders/Penguins	1975–1992, 1993–1994
10.	Nicklas Lidstrom	+450	Red Wings	1991–2012

▲ Bobby Clarke

PLUS/MINUS

SINGLE SEASON

1.	Bobby Orr	+124	Bruins	1970–71
2.	Larry Robinson	+120	Canadiens	1976–77
3.	Wayne Gretzky	+98	Oilers	1984–85
4.	Dallas Smith	+94	Bruins	1970–71
5.	Guy Lafleur	+89	Canadiens	1976–77
6.	Steve Shutt	+88	Canadiens	1976–77
7.	Bobby Orr	+86	Bruins	1971–72
8.	Mark Howe	+85	Flyers	1985–86
9.	Bobby Orr	+84	Bruins	1973–74
10.	Bobby Clarke	+83	Flyers	1975–76
	Brad McCrimmon	+83	Flyers	1985–86

POINTS BY BLADON

Philadelphia Flyers defenseman Tom Bladon had a magical night against the Cleveland Barons in 1977. He scored four goals and assisted on four others. His eight-point game remains the highest-scoring game by an NHL defenseman, equaled later by Paul Coffey of the Edmonton Oilers. But Bladon also set a record for plus/minus that night, finishing with a +10. The Flyers won the game 11-1.

▼ Tom Bladon

RECORD FACT Bill Mikkelson had a tough time in his four seasons in the NHL. He played in 147 career games and was −147 for his career. He holds the record for worst plus-minus in a season with −82 in 1974–75.

🏒 PENALTY MINUTES

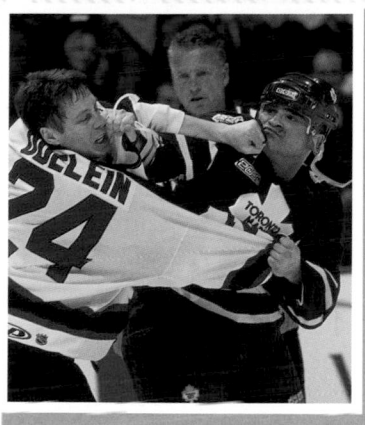

CAREER ||||||||||||||||||||||||||||||||||||||||

1.	Tiger Williams	3,966	Maple Leafs/Canucks/Red Wings/Kings/Whalers	1974–1988
2.	Dale Hunter	3,565	Nordiques/Capitals/Avalanche	1980–1999
3.	Tie Domi	3,515	Maple Leafs/Rangers/Jets	1989–2006
4.	Marty McSorley	3,381	Penguins/Oilers/Kings/Rangers/Sharks/Bruins	1983–2000
5.	Bob Probert	3,300	Red Wings/Blackhawks	1985–2002
6.	Rob Ray	3,207	Sabres/Senators	1989–2004
7.	Craig Berube	3,149	Flyers/Maple Leafs/Flames/Capitals/Islanders	1986–2003
8.	Tim Hunter	3,146	Flames/Nordiques/Canucks/Sharks	1981–1997
9.	Chris Nilan	3,043	Canadiens/Rangers/Bruins	1979–1992
10.	Rick Tocchet	2,972	Flyers/Penguins/Kings/Bruins/Capitals/Coyotes	1984–2002

RECORD FACT

Penalties are measured by minutes. Minor penalties get you two minutes in the penalty box. A major penalty gets you five minutes. A misconduct is worth 10 minutes.

SINGLE SEASON ||||||||||||||||||||||||||||||||||||||||

1.	Dave Schultz	472	Flyers	1974–75
2.	Paul Baxter	409	Penguins	1981–82
3.	Mike Peluso	408	Blackhawks	1991–92
4.	Dave Schultz	405	Kings/Penguins	1977–78
5.	Marty McSorley	399	Kings	1992–93
6.	Bob Probert	398	Red Wings	1987–88
7.	Basil McRae	382	North Stars	1987–88
8.	Joe Kocur	377	Red Wings	1985–86
9.	Tim Hunter	375	Flames	1988–89
10.	Donald Brashear	372	Canucks	1997–98

▲ Dave Schultz

▼ Chris Nilan

ROUGH AND TOUGH

Chris Nilan of the Boston Bruins became the "toughest" player in the NHL on March 31, 1991. The man with the nickname "Knuckles" was penalized a record 10 times for 42 minutes during the game. He was called for six minor penalties, two major penalties, a misconduct, and a game misconduct. Another NHL tough guy, the Los Angeles Kings' Randy Holt, received nine penalties for a record 67 penalty minutes during a game in 1979.

MOST SEASONS ||||||||||||||||||||||||||||||||||||||

1.	Chris Chelios	26	Canadiens/Blackhawks/Red Wings/Thrashers	1983–2010
	Gordie Howe	26	Red Wings/Whalers	1946–1971, 1979–1980
3.	Mark Messier	25	Oilers/Rangers/Canucks	1979–2004
4.	Alex Delvecchio	24	Red Wings	1950–1974
	Tim Horton	24	Maple Leafs/Rangers/Penguins/Sabres	1949–1950, 1951–1974
6.	Five players tied with	23		

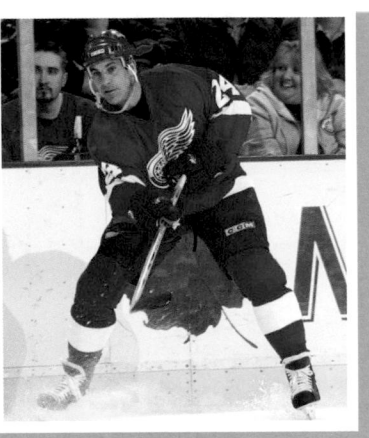
▲ Chris Chelios

RECORD FACT Gordie Howe holds the record for most games played with one franchise. He played in 1,687 games for the Detroit Red Wings.

▼ Mark Recchi

GAMES PLAYED

1.	Gordie Howe	1,767	Red Wings/Whalers	1946–1971, 1979–1980
2.	Mark Messier	1,756	Oilers/Rangers/Canucks	1979–2004
3.	Ron Francis	1,731	Whalers/Penguins/Hurricanes/Maple Leafs	1981–2004
4.	Mark Recchi	1,652	Penguins/Flyers/Canadiens/Hurricanes/Thrashers/Lightning/Bruins	1988–2011
5.	Chris Chelios	1,651	Canadiens/Blackhawks/Red Wings/Thrashers	1983–2010
6.	Dave Andreychuk	1,639	Sabres/Maple Leafs/Devils/Bruins/Avalanche/Lightning	1982–2006
7.	Scott Stevens	1,635	Capitals/Blues/Devils	1982–2004
8.	Larry Murphy	1,615	Kings/Capitals/North Stars/Penguins/Maple Leafs/Red Wings	1980–2001
9.	Ray Bourque	1,612	Bruins/Avalanche	1979–2001
10.	Nicklas Lidstrom	1,564	Red Wings	1991–2012

RECORD FACT Mike Sillinger was a center who played from 1990 to 2009. He played for a record 12 franchises: the Red Wings, Ducks, Canucks, Flyers, Lightning, Panthers, Senators, Blue Jackets, Coyotes, Blues, Predators, and Islanders. Four players tied for second, playing with 10 teams during their careers.

CHAPTER 3

GOALTENDER RECORDS

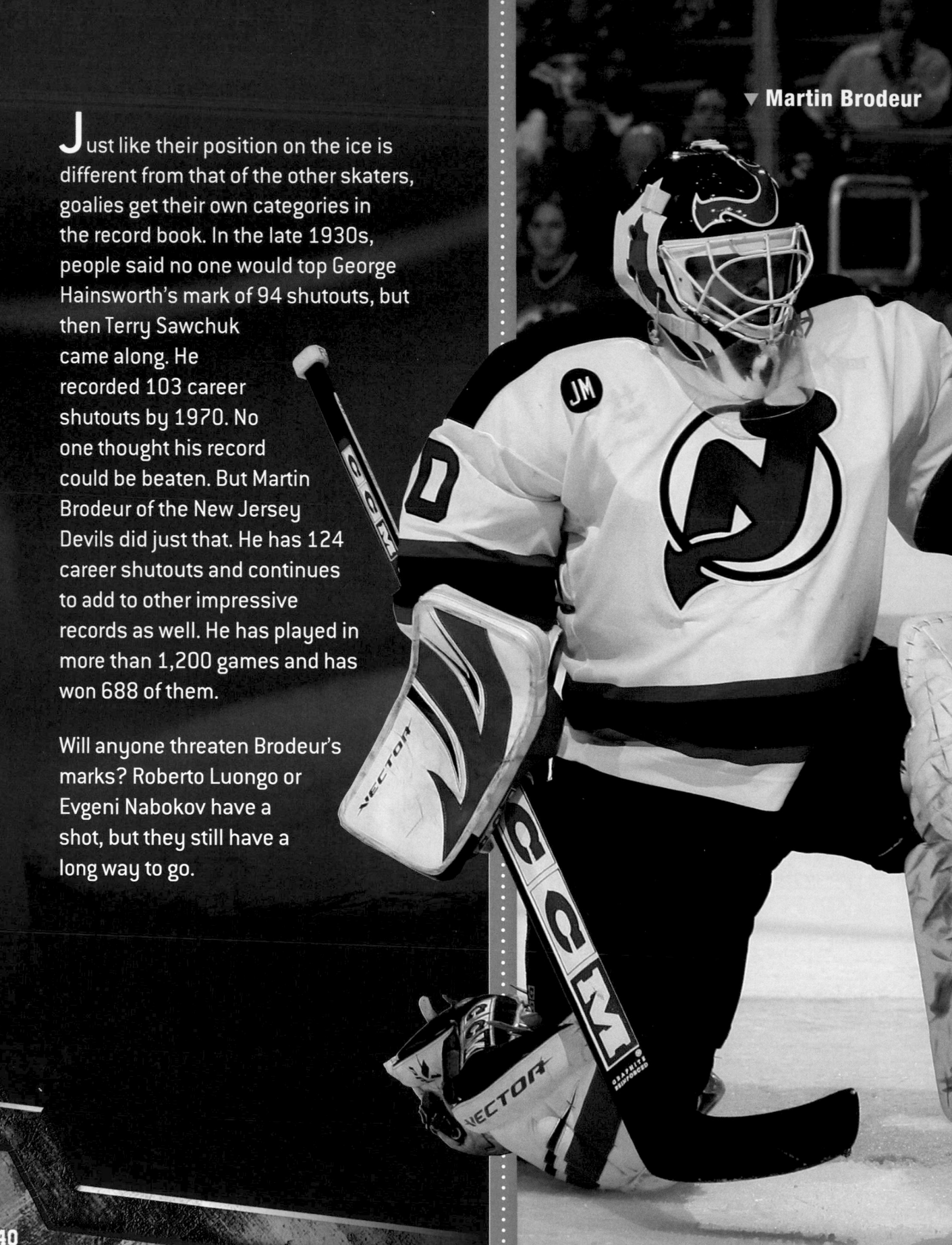

Just like their position on the ice is different from that of the other skaters, goalies get their own categories in the record book. In the late 1930s, people said no one would top George Hainsworth's mark of 94 shutouts, but then Terry Sawchuk came along. He recorded 103 career shutouts by 1970. No one thought his record could be beaten. But Martin Brodeur of the New Jersey Devils did just that. He has 124 career shutouts and continues to add to other impressive records as well. He has played in more than 1,200 games and has won 688 of them.

Will anyone threaten Brodeur's marks? Roberto Luongo or Evgeni Nabokov have a shot, but they still have a long way to go.

WINS

CAREER

1.	Martin Brodeur	688	Devils	1991–1992, 1993–2014*
2.	Patrick Roy	551	Canadiens/ Avalanche	1984–2003
3.	Ed Belfour	484	Blackhawks/Sharks/ Stars/Maple Leafs/ Panthers	1988–1989, 1990–2007
4.	Curtis Joseph	454	Blues/Oilers/Maple Leafs/Red Wings/ Coyotes/Flames	1989–2009
5.	Terry Sawchuk	447	Red Wings/Bruins/ Maple Leafs/Kings/ Rangers	1949–1970
6.	Jacques Plante	437	Canadiens/Rangers/ Blues/Maple Leafs/ Bruins	1952–1965, 1968–1973
7.	Tony Esposito	423	Canadiens/ Blackhawks	1968–1984
8.	Glenn Hall	407	Red Wings/ Blackhawks/Blues	1952–1953, 1954–1971
9.	Grant Fuhr	403	Oilers/Maple Leafs/ Sabres/Kings/ Blues/Flames	1981–2000
10.	Chris Osgood	401	Red Wings/ Islanders/Blues/	1993–2011

*Active player

RECORD FACT Martin Brodeur holds the record for career losses with 394. Goalies Gump Worsley and Curtis Joseph come in second with 352 losses each. Gary Smith of the California Golden Seals holds the record for most losses in a single season with 48 in 1970–71.

 **WINS**

▼ Roberto Luongo

SINGLE SEASON				
1.	Martin Brodeur	48	Devils	2006–07
2.	Bernie Parent	47	Flyers	1973–74
	Roberto Luongo	47	Canucks	2006–07
4.	Evgeni Nabokov	46	Sharks	2007–08
5.	Martin Brodeur	45	Devils	2009–10
	Miikka Kiprusoff	45	Flames	2008–09
7.	Martin Brodeur	44	Devils	2007–08
	Evgeni Nabokov	44	Sharks	2009–10
	Bernie Parent	44	Flyers	1974–75
	Terry Sawchuk	44	Red Wings	1950–51
	Terry Sawchuk	44	Red Wings	1951–52

KEEP ON WINNIN'

Gilles Gilbert of the Boston Bruins holds the record for consecutive victories. He won 17 straight games in 1975–76. The Bruins' Gerry Cheevers has the record for the longest undefeated streak, going 24–0–8 in 1971–72. (The NHL had ties before introducing the shootout in 2005.)

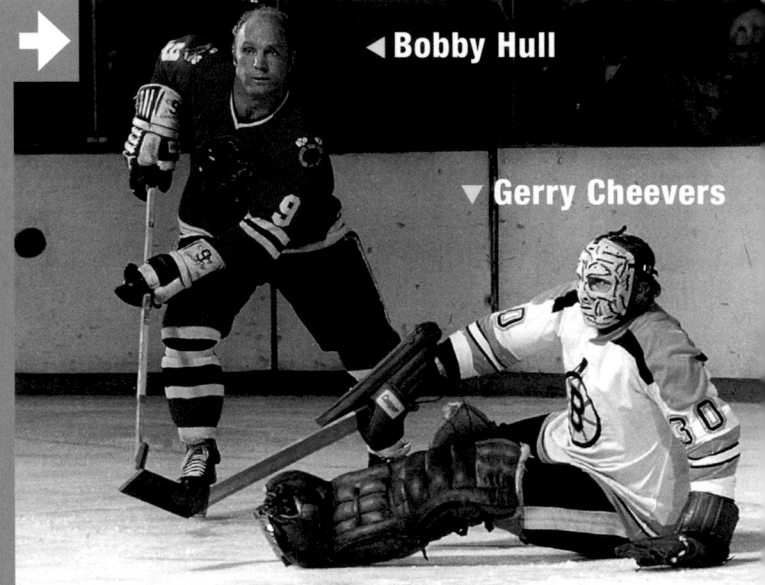
◀ Bobby Hull

▼ Gerry Cheevers

RECORD FACT Goals-against average is a stat that shows how many goals per game are allowed by the goalie on average. To find the goals-against average, take the number of goals allowed and multiply by 60. Then divide the result by the number of minutes played.

GOALS-AGAINST AVERAGE

CAREER

1.	Alec Connell	1.91	Senators/Falcons/Americans/Maroons	1924–1935, 1936–1937
2.	George Hainsworth	1.93	Canadiens/Maple Leafs	1926–1937
3.	Charlie Gardiner	2.02	Blackhawks	1927–1934
4.	Lorne Chabot	2.03	Rangers/Maple Leafs/Canadiens/Blackhawks/Maroons/Americans	1926–1937
5.	Tiny Thompson	2.08	Bruins/Red Wings	1928–1940
6.	Dave Kerr	2.15	Maroons/Americans/Rangers	1930–1941
7.	Dominik Hasek	2.20	Blackhawks/Sabres/Red Wings/Senators	1990–1995, 1996–2002, 2006–2008
8.	Martin Brodeur	2.24	Devils	1991–1992, 1993–2014*
	Ken Dryden	2.24	Canadiens	1970–1973, 1974–1979
10.	Henrik Lundqvist	2.26	Rangers	2005–2014*

*Active player

SINGLE SEASON

1.	George Hainsworth	0.92	Canadiens	1928–29
2.	George Hainsworth	1.06	Canadiens	1927–28
3.	Alec Connell	1.12	Senators	1925–26
4.	Tiny Thompson	1.15	Bruins	1928–29
5.	Roy Worters	1.16	Americans	1928–29
6.	Alec Connell	1.24	Senators	1927–28
7.	Dolly Dolson	1.38	Cougars	1928–29
8.	John Ross Roach	1.41	Rangers	1928–29
9.	Clint Benedict	1.42	Maroons	1926–27
10.	Alec Connell	1.43	Senators	1928–29

▲ Tiny Thompson

SHUTOUTS

▼ Jacques Plante

CAREER ||||||||||||||||||||||||||||||||||||||||||||||

1.	Martin Brodeur	124	Devils	1991–1992, 1993–2014*
2.	Terry Sawchuk	103	Red Wings/Bruins/ Maple Leafs/Kings/ Rangers	1949–1970
3.	George Hainsworth	94	Canadiens/Maple Leafs	1926–1937
4.	Glenn Hall	84	Red Wings/ Blackhawks/Blues	1952–1953, 1954–1971
5.	Jacques Plante	82	Canadiens/Rangers/ Blues/Maple Leafs/ Bruins	1952–1965, 1968–1973
6.	Alec Connell	81	Senators/Falcons/ Americans/Maroons	1924–1935, 1936–1937
	Dominik Hasek	81	Blackhawks/Sabres/ Red Wings/Senators	1990–1995, 1996–2002, 2006–2008
	Tiny Thompson	81	Bruins/Red Wings	1928–1940
9.	Ed Belfour	76	Blackhawks/Sharks/ Stars/Maple Leafs/ Panthers	1988–1989, 1990–2007
	Tony Esposito	76	Canadiens/ Blackhawks	1968–1940

*Active player

SINGLE SEASON ||||||||||||||||||||||||||||||||||||||||||||

1.	George Hainsworth	22	Canadiens	1928–29
2.	Alec Connell	15	Senators	1925–26
	Alec Connell	15	Senators	1927–28
	Tony Esposito	15	Blackhawks	1969–70
	Hal Winkler	15	Bruins	1927–28
6.	George Hainsworth	14	Canadiens	1926–27
7.	Seven players tied with	13		

GOALS FOR GOALIES

Goalies usually miss out on the glory of scoring a goal. But goalies have proven they can score too. Ten goaltenders have been credited with scoring goals. For some, they were simply the last offensive player to touch the puck before a defensive player put the puck in his own net. However, some have shot and scored into an open net. In 2013 Martin Brodeur became the first goaltender to be credited for a third goal.

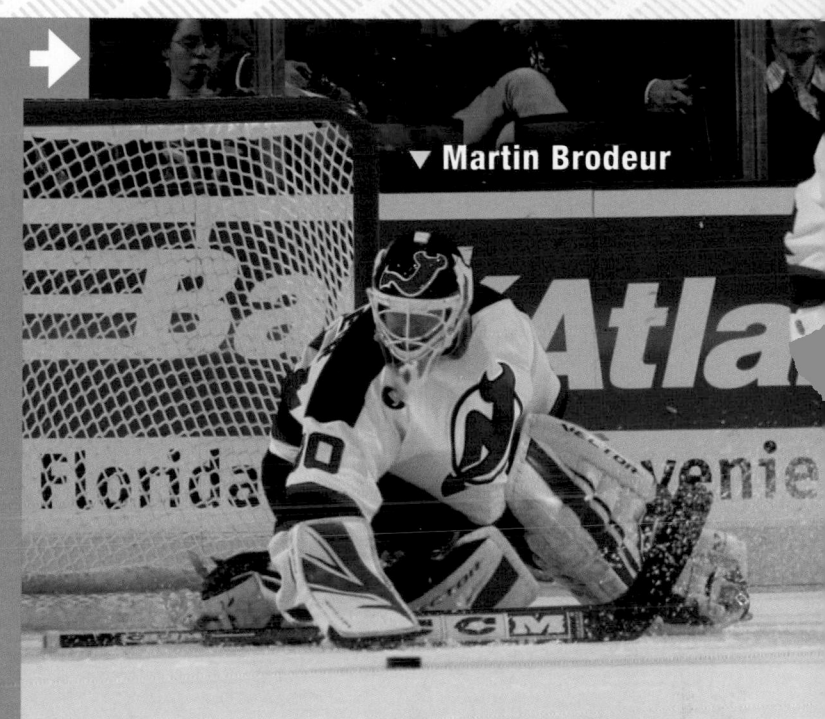

▼ Martin Brodeur

▼ Jose Theodore

GOAL-SCORING GOALIES		
Billy Smith	Islanders	Nov. 28, 1979
Ron Hextall	Flyers	Dec. 8, 1987
Ron Hextall	Flyers	April 11, 1989
Chris Osgood	Red Wings	March 6, 1996
Martin Brodeur	Devils	April 17, 1997
Damian Rhodes	Senators	Jan. 2, 1999
Martin Brodeur	Devils	Feb. 15, 2000
Jose Theodore	Canadiens	Jan. 2, 2001
Evgeni Nabokov	Sharks	March 10, 2002
Mika Noronen	Sabres	Feb. 14, 2004
Chris Mason	Predators	April 15, 2006
Cam Ward	Hurricanes	Dec. 26, 2011
Martin Brodeur	Devils	March 21, 2013

RECORD FACT

In 1993 the Calgary Flames defeated the San Jose Sharks 13-1. Goaltender Jeff Reese assisted on three of the goals No other goalie has had a three-point game.

FORWARDS

Forwards skate up front and get down deep. These right wings, left wings, and centers are the driving force behind putting points on the scoreboard. If the forwards don't start the offense, they usually finish it with nifty passes and gritty goals.

WAYNE GRETZKY

Wayne Gretzky's records will likely stand for a long time. "The Great One" was the only player to score more than 200 points in a single season—a feat he accomplished four times. His best season was 1985–1986 when he scored 52 goals and had 163 assists for 215 points. In 1981–1982 he scored a record 92 goals. For his career, Gretzky recorded 2,857 points, but his 1,963 assists alone would put him at the top of the all-time scoring list. The NHL retired Gretzky's 99 jersey number, meaning no player from any team can wear the number.

GORDIE HOWE

Gordie Howe was called Mr. Hockey for a good reason. He led the NHL in points six times, but he was also known for his rough-and-tumble play. Any player who scores a goal, gets an assist, and gets in a fight achieves a "Gordie Howe hat trick." Howe played professional hockey until 1980 at age 51. During his final three seasons, he played for the New England Whalers along with his sons, Mark and Marty. In 1997, when Howe was 69 years old, the Detroit Vipers of the International Hockey League signed him to play in one game, making Howe the first professional hockey player to play in six different decades.

MARIO LEMIEUX

Who knows how many points "Super" Mario Lemieux would have scored had he been healthy for his entire career. Still, a battle with cancer and back surgery couldn't keep the Pittsburgh star sidelined for good. Three years after retiring, being inducted into the Hall of Fame, and becoming part-owner of the Penguins, he made a comeback and played five more seasons for Pittsburgh. Lemieux is the only person in history to win a Stanley Cup as a player and as an owner.

Top Forwards

- Jean Beliveau, Canadiens—named to 13 All-Star Games
- Wayne Gretzky, Oilers/Kings/Blues/Rangers—hockey's all-time leading scorer
- Gordie Howe, Red Wings/Houston Aeros/Whalers—played 32 seasons of professional hockey
- Bobby Hull, Blackhawks/Jets/Whalers—four-time MVP (two in NHL, two in the World Hockey Association)
- Guy Lafleur, Canadiens/Rangers/Nordiques—two-time MVP
- Mario Lemieux, Penguins—won three MVP awards
- Mark Messier, Oilers/Rangers/Canucks/Indianapolis Racers/Stingers—named to 15 All-Star Games
- Stan Mikita, Blackhawks—four-time scoring leader
- Howie Morenz, Canadiens/Blackhawks/Rangers—three-time MVP
- Maurice Richard, Canadiens—led Montreal to eight Stanley Cup wins

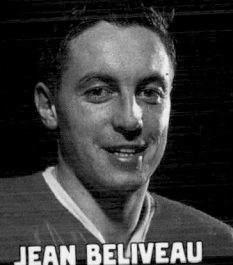
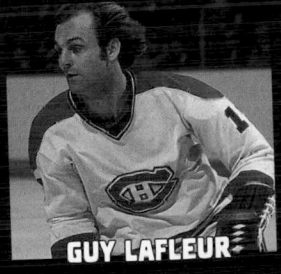
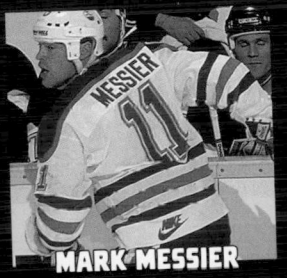

JEAN BELIVEAU   GUY LAFLEUR   MARK MESSIER   MAURICE RICHARD

DEFENSEMEN

They're known as the blue liners and are often the last line of defense before the goaltender. But defensemen do much more than take on the other team's forwards. The best defenders can score too.

SCOTT NIEDERMAYER

BOBBY ORR

Bobby Orr changed the defenseman position forever in the NHL. There were offensive defensemen before Orr, but few could skate or handle the puck like him. During one penalty kill, he skated for 21 seconds without losing the puck before scoring a short-handed goal. He was named the NHL's MVP three times in his career.

CHRIS CHELIOS

You can't keep Chris Chelios down. After playing more than 24 seasons in the NHL, he played minor-league hockey from 2008 to 2010. Then the NHL called him one more time. In 2009–2010, at the age of 48, he played seven games for the Atlanta Thrashers before retiring in August. No defenseman has played in more NHL games than Chelios. In fact, only three other players—all forwards—have played more.

DOUG HARVEY

Doug Harvey was a big reason why the Montreal Canadiens won five Stanley Cups in a row from 1956–1960. He was a great defender who blocked shots and moved the puck out of his team's end. He also excelled on power plays and passing the puck to his high-scoring teammates. Harvey won the Norris Trophy as the NHL's best defenseman seven times. Only Bobby Orr has won the award more times.

Top Defensemen

- Ray Bourque, Bruins/Avalanche—voted to 19 All-Star Games
- Chris Chelios, Canadiens/Blackhawks/Red Wings/Thrashers—played 26 seasons in the league
- Paul Coffey, Oilers/Penguins/Kings/Red Wings/Whalers/Flyers/Blackhawks/Hurricanes/Bruins—ranks second among defensemen in career goals (396)
- Doug Harvey, Canadiens/Rangers/Red Wings/Blues—13-time All-Star Game pick
- Red Kelly, Red Wings/Maple Leafs—selected for the All-Star Game 12 times
- Nicklas Lidstrom, Red Wings—11-time All Star won the Norris Trophy seven times
- Bobby Orr, Bruins/Blackhawks—named NHL's best defenseman eight times
- Denis Potvin, Islanders—named league's best defenseman three times
- Larry Robinson, Canadiens/Kings—twice named league's best defenseman
- Eddie Shore, Bruins/New York Americans—four-time MVP

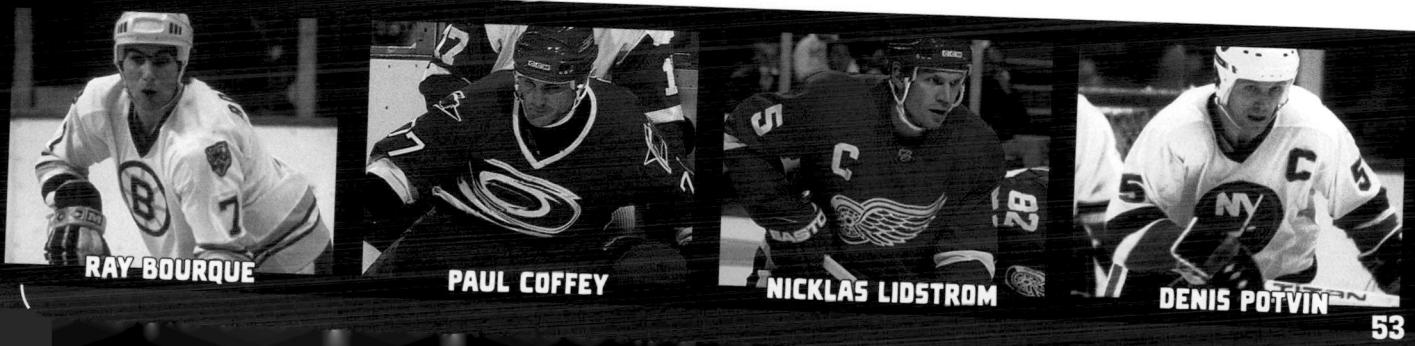

RAY BOURQUE   PAUL COFFEY   NICKLAS LIDSTROM   DENIS POTVIN

GOALTENDERS

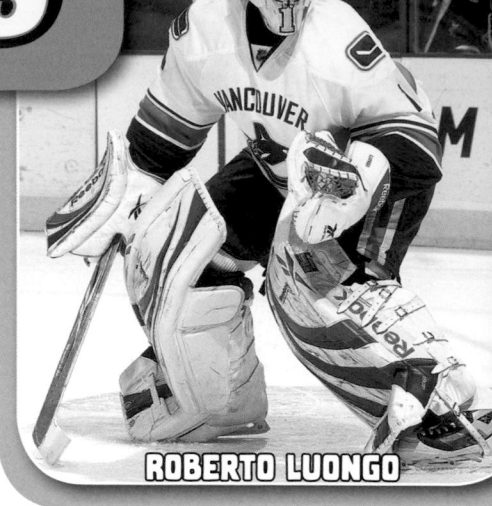

ROBERTO LUONGO

Goaltenders play one of the toughest positions in any sport. They need eagle eyes and catlike reflexes to stop speedy slap shots, wicked wristers, and tricky tip-ins.

PATRICK ROY

You couldn't script a better full first season than the one Patrick Roy had. By the time the 1986 playoffs started during his rookie year, he was the Canadiens' number one goalie. He led the team all the way to the Stanley Cup championship. He allowed fewer than two goals per game during the playoffs and won the Conn Smythe Award as the playoff MVP. Over the next 17 seasons, "St. Patrick" won three more titles—one with Montreal and two with the Colorado Avalanche.

MARTIN BRODEUR

Patrick Roy's records seemed unbreakable when he retired in 2003, but Martin Brodeur proved he was up to the task. Drafted in 1990, he has spent his entire career with the New Jersey Devils. He has won three Stanley Cups and owns some of the game's most spectacular saves with his unique defensive style. Brodeur has more wins (688) and more shutouts (124) than any other goalie in league history.

JACQUES PLANTE

Jacques Plante's influence on the game is still felt today. He was the first NHL goaltender to regularly wear a mask to protect his face from flying pucks, although others had tried it briefly. Even though his coach didn't like the look at first, Plante kept the mask as the Canadiens won 18 games in a row. He won six Stanley Cups and was one of the few goaltenders to win the Hart Trophy as league MVP.

Top Goaltenders

- Turk Broda, Maple Leafs—led Toronto to five championships
- Martin Brodeur, Devils—owns most of the NHL's career goalie records
- Ken Dryden, Canadiens—won six Stanley Cups in eight-year career
- Bill Durnan, Canadiens—voted NHL's top goalie six times
- George Hainsworth, Canadiens/Maple Leafs—voted league's best goalie three times
- Dominik Hasek, Blackhawks/Sabres/Red Wings/Senators—only goalie to win two MVPs
- Jacques Plante, Canadiens/Rangers/Blues/Maple Leafs/Bruins/Oilers—led Montreal to five Cup wins in a row
- Patrick Roy, Canadiens/Avalanche—playoff MVP in three of his four Stanley Cup wins
- Terry Sawchuk, Red Wings/Bruins/Maple Leafs/Kings/Rangers—voted top goalie four times

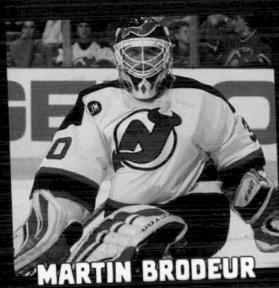

MARTIN BRODEUR

KEN DRYDEN

DOMINIK HASEK

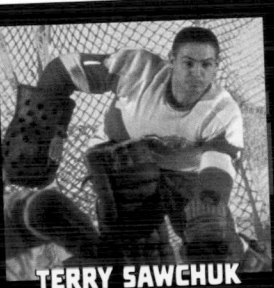

TERRY SAWCHUK

CURRENT & RISING STARS

The NHL has had a legendary past, but it also has a bright future. The league currently has several players striving for the Hall of Fame. From Joe Thornton to Sidney Crosby, these stars add an exciting spark to pro hockey.

SIDNEY CROSBY

Few players have burst onto the hockey scene like Pittsburgh Penguins star Sidney Crosby. "Sid the Kid" was only 19 years old when he was named the team captain—at the time the youngest captain in NHL history. He also became the league's youngest scoring champion and the second-youngest MVP after Wayne Gretzky. In 2014 he won the Hart trophy as MVP for the second time.

ALEX OVECHKIN

It didn't take long for Alex Ovechkin to become a superstar. In 2006 the Russian left wing won the Calder Trophy as rookie of the year. Two seasons later he was the league MVP, winning the first of three Hart Trophies. He scored 50 or more goals and more than 100 points in four of his first five seasons. In 2014, he scored his 400th goal, becoming the sixth-fastest player to reach that milestone.

HENRIK AND DANIEL SEDIN

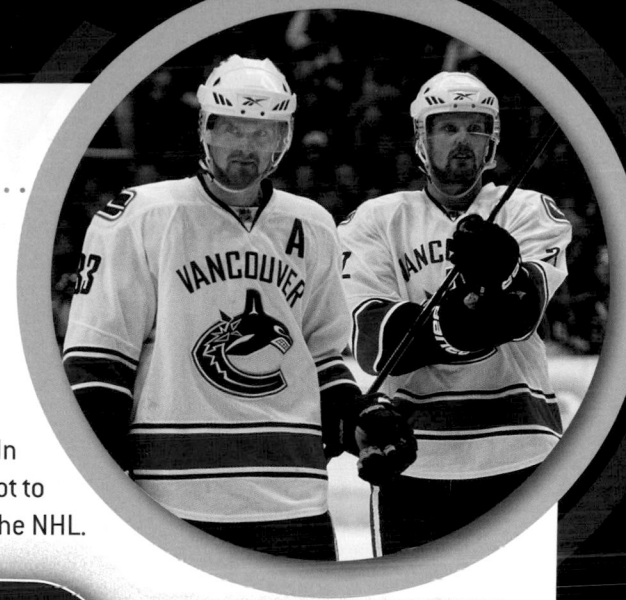

Two of the best players in the NHL are twin brothers Henrik (left) and Daniel Sedin of the Vancouver Canucks. In 1999 the Canucks made a trade to get the second- and third-overall picks in the summer draft and took the Sedin twins. Through their first 13 seasons, Daniel has 307 goals and 805 points, and Henrik has 193 goals and 842 points. In 2010 Henrik led the NHL with 83 assists and 112 points. Not to be outdone, Daniel scored 104 points in 2011, the best in the NHL.

Top Current & Rising Stars

- Drew Doughty, D, Kings—Key figure on Los Angeles's 2012 ans 2014 championships
- Patrick Kane, F, Blackhawks—2008 rookie of the year and three-time All-Star
- Erik Karlsson, D, Senators—Top-scoring defenseman in two of his first five seasons
- Evgeni Malkin, F, Penguins— 2007 rookie of the year and 2012 MVP
- Rick Nash, F, Blue Jackets/Rangers—has been selected to the All-Star Game five times
- Jonathan Quick, G, Kings—backstopped championships in 2012 and 2014
- Steven Stamkos, F, Lightning—two-time league leader in goal scoring
- P.K. Subban, D, Canadiens—named the league's best defenseman in 2013
- John Tavares, F, Islanders—NHL's first overall draft pick in 2009
- Jonathan Toews, F, Blackhawks—captained Chicago to Stanley Cup wins in 2010 and 2013

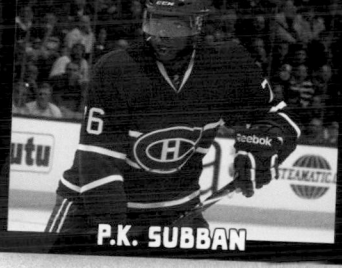

P.K. SUBBAN

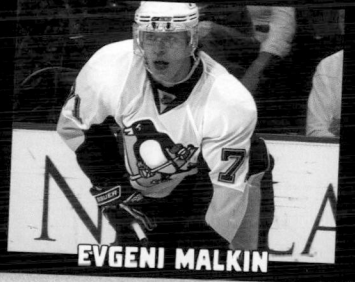

EVGENI MALKIN

JONATHAN QUICK

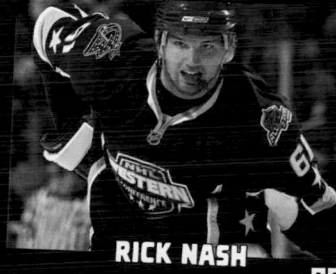

RICK NASH

MVPS

After every season the NHL awards the Hart Trophy to the season's best player. It is the league's most valuable player award, and it has gone to some great hockey stars.

TRADED **AWAY**

During the 2005–2006 season, the Boston Bruins sent Joe Thornton all the way across the country, trading him to the San Jose Sharks. Thornton joined a team that was 8–12–4 and had lost 10 games in a row. But he led the Sharks to a 36–15–7 record the rest of the way. Thornton was the only player in NHL history to be traded during the season in which he won the MVP.

GREATNESS

HAS HART

The great Wayne Gretzky won nine Hart Trophies, including an amazing eight in a row from 1980 to 1987 with the Edmonton Oilers. In 1989, after "the trade of the century" sent Gretzky to the Kings, he won his final MVP award. Mario Lemieux broke up Gretzky's streak after a 168-point season in 1988–1989, winning the first of his three Hart Trophies.

GOALIES ARE VALUABLE TOO

Goaltenders have their own postseason awards, but they have also been voted as the MVP seven times in NHL history. The first goalie to receive the award was the New York Americans' Roy Worters in 1929. In 1997 the Sabres' Dominik Hasek became the first goalie since Jacques Plante in 1962 to be named MVP. He won the award again the following year, becoming the only goalie to win the award twice. The most recent goalie to win the award was the Canadiens' Jose Theodore in 2002.

MULTIPLE MVP WINNERS

Player	Team	Awards
Wayne Gretzky	Oilers/Kings	9
Gordie Howe	Red Wings	6
Eddie Shore	Bruins	4
Bobby Clarke	Flyers	3
Mario Lemieux	Penguins	3
Howie Morenz	Canadiens	3
Bobby Orr	Bruins	3
Alex Ovechkin	Capitals	3
Jean Beliveau	Canadiens	2
Bill Cowley	Bruins	2
Phil Esposito	Bruins	2
Dominik Hasek	Sabres	2
Bobby Hull	Blackhawks/Blues	2
Guy Lafleur	Canadiens	2
Mark Messier	Rangers/Oilers	2
Stan Mikita	Blackhawks	2
Nels Stewart	Maroons	2
Sidney Crosby	Penguins	2

DREAM TEAM

Imagine a team made up of the greatest players who ever skated onto a hockey rink. Few would argue that Wayne Gretzky should be the number one center. But from there picking the lineup would be almost impossible. Is Martin Brodeur the best goalie, or is Patrick Roy? How do you choose between Nicklas Lidstrom and Chris Chelios on defense? Is Bobby Hull the best left wing of all time? Is Brett Hull the best right wing?

Most hockey teams play with four forward lines consisting of a center, left wing, and right wing, three defensive pairs, and up to three goalies.

IF YOU WERE THE COACH, WHO WOULD YOU PICK FOR YOUR TEAM?

Left Wing

Bobby Hull, Blackhawks

Alex Ovechkin, Capitals

Luc Robitaille, Kings

Frank Mahovlich, Maple Leafs

Right Wing

Gordie Howe, Red Wings

Maurice Richard, Canadiens

Mike Bossy, Islanders

Brett Hull, Blues

Center

Wayne Gretzky, Oilers

Mario Lemieux, Penguins

Mark Messier, Oilers

Jean Beliveau, Canadiens

Goaltender

Patrick Roy, Avalanche

Martin Brodeur, Devils

Terry Sawchuk, Red Wings

Defenseman

Bobby Orr, Bruins

Doug Harvey, Canadiens

Ray Bourque, Bruins

Nicklas Lidstrom, Red Wings

Eddie Shore, Bruins

Denis Potvin, Islanders

CURRENT VS. CLASSIC

What was the best era of the NHL? The days when only the Original Six teams existed? The rough-and-tough days of the 1970s? Are we seeing it today? Can you even compare various periods of the NHL? Look at some of today's stars matched up against some of yesterday's best. Who do you think is better?

LEFT WING

Alex Ovechkin, Capitals	Bobby Hull, Blackhawks/ Jets/Whalers*
6 feet 2 inches (188 cm)	5 feet 10 inches (178 cm)
223 pounds (101 kg)	195 pounds (88 kg)
2005–present	1957–1980
422 goals	913 goals
392 assists	895 assists
814 points	1,808 points
456 penalty minutes	823 penalty minutes

RIGHT WING

Jarome Iginla, Flames/Penguins/Bruins	Gordie Howe, Red Wings/ Aeros/Whalers*
6 feet 1 inch (185 cm)	6 feet (183 cm)
207 pounds (94 kg)	205 pounds (93 kg)
1996–present	1946–1980
560 goals	975 goals
607 assists	1,383 assists
1,157 points	2,358 points
887 penalty minutes	2,084 penalty minutes

JAROME IGINLA

All stats are through the 2012–13 season.

CENTER

Sidney Crosby, Penguins		Wayne Gretzky, Oilers/Kings/Blues/Rangers*
5 feet 11 inches (180 cm) 200 pounds (91 kg)	⊢⊣	6 feet (183 cm) 185 pounds (84 kg)
2005–present	⊢⊣	1978–1999
274 goals 495 assists 769 points 463 penalty minutes	⊢⊣	940 goals 2,027 assists 2,967 points 596 penalty minutes

SIDNEY CROSBY

DEFENSEMAN

Duncan Keith, Blackhawks		Bobby Orr, Bruins/Blackhawks
6 feet 1 inch (185 cm) 196 pounds (89 kg)	⊢⊣	6 feet (183 cm) 197 pounds (89 kg)
2005–present	⊢⊣	1966–1979
65 goals 305 assists 370 points 445 penalty minutes	⊢⊣	270 goals 645 assists 915 points 953 penalty minutes

TERRY SAWCHUK

GOALTENDER

Martin Brodeur, Devils		Terry Sawchuk, Red Wings/Bruins/Maple Leafs/Kings/Rangers
6 feet 2 inches (188 cm) 215 pounds (98 kg)	⊢⊣	5 feet 11 inches (180 cm) 195 pounds (88 kg)
1991–present	⊢⊣	1949–1970
688 wins 2.24 goals-against average	⊢⊣	447 wins 2.51 goals-against average

*combined NHL/WHA stats

CHAPTER 5

TEAM RECORDS

Hockey is considered to be one of the greatest team games. Goals are rarely scored without help—that's why assists are awarded. Goaltenders are aided by their defensemen and forwards' strong play at their own end of the rink. If it's all done well together, a team will be successful. The team's going to score goals. It's going to limit opponents' scoring chances. It's going to win games. And it has a chance to set records.

The best teams hold records for the most championships, the most wins, and the most points. Can you imagine what it would have been like to be an Edmonton Oilers fan in the 1980s? For five years in a row, they not only led the league in scoring, but they hit goal totals never seen before or since in NHL history. During the 1983–84 season, Edmonton scored 446 goals. In comparison, in 2011–12, the Pittsburgh Pengiuns led the league with 273 goals—173 fewer than the highest-scoring team of all time.

MOST WINS (SINGLE SEASON) ||||||||||||

1.	Detroit Red Wings	62	1995–96
2.	Montreal Canadiens	60	1976–77
3.	Montreal Canadiens	59	1977–78
4.	Detroit Red Wings	58	2005–06
	Montreal Canadiens	58	1975–76
6.	Boston Bruins	57	1970–71
	Edmonton Oilers	57	1983–84
8.	Edmonton Oilers	56	1985–86
	Pittsburgh Penguins	56	1992–93
10.	Eight teams tied with	54	

▲ Sergei Fedorov of the
Detroit Red Wings

FEWEST WINS (SINGLE SEASON) ||||||||||||

1.	Washington Capitals	8	1974–75
2.	Winnipeg Jets	9	1980–81
3.	Ottawa Senators	10	1992–93
4.	San Jose Sharks	11	1992–93
	Washington Capitals	11	1975–76
6.	Chicago Blackhawks	12	1953–54
	Kansas City Scouts	12	1975–76
	New York Islanders	12	1972–73
	Quebec Nordiques	12	1989–90
10.	Three teams tied with	13	

▲ Robert Picard of the
Washington Capitals

RECORD FACT The most- and fewest-wins records come from the era in which the NHL played 70 games or more. The NHL schedule expanded from 60 to 70 games starting with the 1949–50 season.

▼ **Philadelphia Flyers**

Winning Streak: The Pittsburgh Penguins won 17 games in a row during the 1992–93 season.

Unbeaten Streak: The Philadelphia Flyers did not lose a game in 35 straight contests during the 1979–80 season, going 25–0–10.

Losing Streak: The longest losing streak is 17 games in a row, set by the Washington Capitals in 1974–75 and the San Jose Sharks in 1992–93.

Winless Streak: The Winnipeg Jets went 0–23–7, a streak of 30 games in a row without a win in the 1980–81 season.

MOST GOALS SCORED IN A SEASON ||||||||||||||||||||||||

1.	Edmonton Oilers	446	1983–84
2	Edmonton Oilers	426	1985–86
3.	Edmonton Oilers	424	1982–83
4.	Edmonton Oilers	417	1981–82
5.	Edmonton Oilers	401	1984–85
6.	Boston Bruins	399	1970–71
7.	Calgary Flames	397	1987–88
8.	Montreal Canadiens	387	1976–77
9.	New York Islanders	385	1981–82
10.	Los Angeles Kings	376	1988–89

▲ **Wayne Gretzky of the Edmonton Oilers**

RECORD FACT Only one team in NHL history has averaged less than one goal per game on offense. The 1928–29 Chicago Blackhawks scored just 33 goals in a 44-game season, an average of 0.75 goals per game.

MOST GOALS ALLOWED IN A SEASON

1.	Washington Capitals	446	1974–75
2.	Detroit Red Wings	415	1985–86
3.	San Jose Sharks	414	1992–93
4.	Quebec Nordiques	407	1989–90
5.	Hartford Whalers	403	1982–83
6.	Vancouver Canucks	401	1984–85
7.	Winnipeg Jets	400	1980–81
8.	Ottawa Senators	397	1993–94
9.	Ottawa Senators	395	1992–93
10.	Washington Capitals	394	1975–76
	Pittsburgh Penguins	394	1982–83

RECORD FACT The Montreal Canadiens defeated the Quebec Bulldogs 16-3 on March 3, 1920. No team since has scored 16 goals in a single game.

MOST GOALS IN A GAME (BOTH TEAMS)

1.	Canadiens 14, St. Patricks 7	21	Jan. 10, 1920
	Oilers 12, Blackhawks 9	21	Dec. 11, 1985
3.	Oilers 12, North Stars 8	20	Jan. 4, 1984
	Maple Leafs 11, Oilers 9	20	Jan. 8, 1986
5.	Wanderers 10, Arenas 9	19	Dec. 19, 1917
	Canadiens 16, Bulldogs 3	19	March 3, 1920
	Canadiens 13, Tigers 6	19	Feb. 26, 1921
	Bruins 10, Rangers 9	19	March 4, 1944
	Red Wings 10, Bruins 9	19	March 16, 1944
	Canucks 10, North Stars 9	19	Oct. 7, 1983

SINGLE-PERIOD SCORING

The Buffalo Sabres set the record for most goals by a team in one period on March 19, 1981. In a 14-4 victory over the Toronto Maple Leafs, Buffalo scored nine goals in the second period. Toronto also scored three times that period. The 12 combined goals are tied for a record with the Edmonton Oilers and Chicago Blackhawks. The two teams each had six goals in a period during a 1985 game.

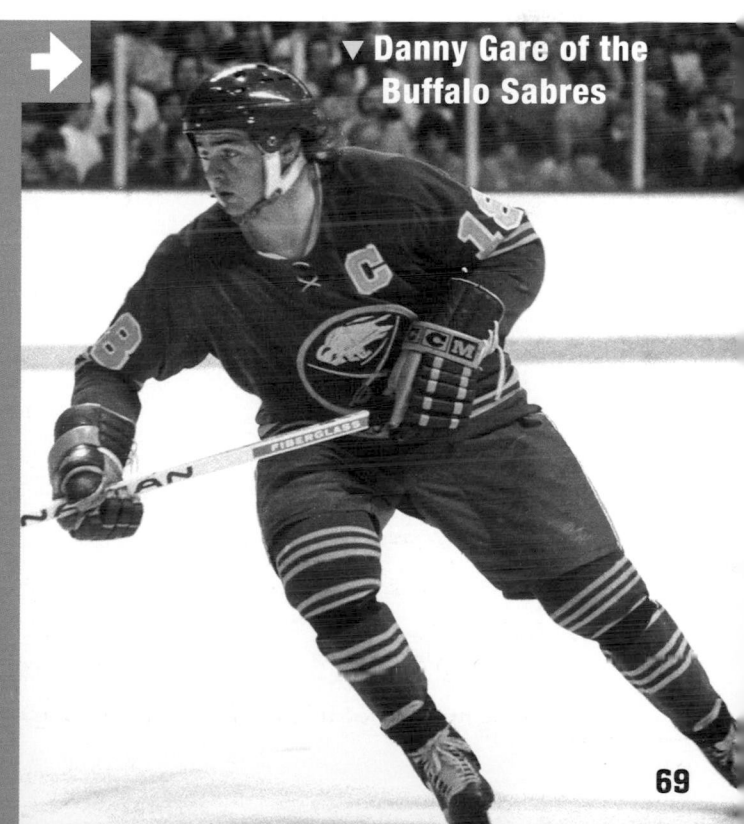

▼ Danny Gare of the Buffalo Sabres

CHAPTER 6

THE TEAMS

For many years there were only six teams in the NHL: the Boston Bruins, Chicago Blackhawks, Detroit Red Wings, Montreal Canadiens, New York Rangers, and Toronto Maple Leafs. In 1967 the league doubled in size. Over the next 33 years, 18 more teams joined the league, putting pro hockey in almost every major city in North America.

EASTERN CONFERENCE

Metropolitan Division

Carolina Hurricanes—In 1997 the Hurricanes moved from Hartford, Connecticut—where they were the Whalers—to Raleigh, North Carolina.

Columbus Blue Jackets—The Blue Jackets became Ohio's second NHL team when they joined the league in 2000; the Cleveland Barons lasted just two seasons before the franchise moved in the 1970s.

New Jersey Devils—The Devils started out in Kansas City as the Scouts before moving to Colorado as the Rockies and finally to New Jersey.

New York Islanders—The Islanders' Mike Bossy had nine 50-goal seasons for New York; he is the only player in history to have that many with the same team.

New York Rangers—The Rangers were not the first NHL team to play in New York City, but they survived after the New York/Brooklyn Americans folded.

Philadelphia Flyers—The NHL doubled in size, going from six teams to 12 in 1967. In 1974 the Flyers became the first of those new teams to win the Stanley Cup.

Pittsburgh Penguins—When Mario Lemieux came out of retirement in 2000, he became the first team owner to skate in an NHL game.

Washington Capitals—The Capitals' first season, 1974–1975, was the worst for any team in NHL history; they had a .131 winning percentage and lost 17 games in a row during one stretch.

Atlantic Division

Boston Bruins—The Bruins were the first U.S. team to join the NHL, which only had Canadian teams at the time.

Buffalo Sabres—The NHL decided to expand into Buffalo, New York, in 1970; the decision was based on the success of a minor-league team that played in that city for 30 years and won five championships.

Detroit Red Wings—Detroit's NHL team was called the Cougars for four years and then the Falcons for two years before settling on the Red Wings in 1932.

Florida Panthers—The Panthers won 33 games during their first season (1993–1994) in Florida, a record for an expansion team.

Montreal Canadiens—Only Major League Baseball's New York Yankees have won more professional championships (27) than the Canadiens, who have 24 Stanley Cups.

Ottawa Senators—The original Ottawa Senators existed from the late 1800s to 1935. In 1992 the NHL added a new team with the old name in Canada's capital city.

Tampa Bay Lightning—When they won the 2004 Cup, the Lightning became the southern-most team in the NHL to win a championship.

Toronto Maple Leafs—The Leafs were first called the Arenas and the St. Patricks before they got their current nickname in 1926.

Central Division

Chicago Blackhawks—In 1937–1938 the Blackhawks went 14–25–9, yet won the Stanley Cup; it remains the worst record of any championship team.

Colorado Avalanche—The Avalanche won the Stanley Cup in 1995–1996, their first year in Denver after moving from Quebec City, where they were the Nordiques.

Dallas Stars—Mike Modano spent 20 seasons with the Stars—four when the team was in Minnesota—and became the NHL's top-scoring U.S.-born player.

Minnesota Wild—Before the first home game in franchise history, the Wild retired the number 1 in honor of their fans, who were without an NHL team for seven years.

Nashville Predators—The Predators got their nickname because the bones of a saber-toothed tiger were found in an underground cave near Nashville, Tennessee.

St. Louis Blues—The Blues played in the Stanley Cup finals in each of their first three seasons, losing to the Canadiens in 1968 and 1969 and the Bruins in 1970.

Winnipeg Jets—The Winnipeg Jets name resurfaced in 2012 when the Atlanta Thrashers moved to Winnipeg, Manitoba, Canada. The original Jets moved to Phoenix.

Pacific Division

Anaheim Ducks—The team was originally called the Mighty Ducks, named after a 1992 Disney movie about a youth hockey team.

Arizona Coyotes—Phoenix is one of many teams with a connection to Wayne Gretzky; he coached the Coyotes for four seasons and was once a partial owner of the Arizona team.

Calgary Flames—Three brothers from the Sutter family have coached the Flames: Brent, Brian, and Darryl; another brother—Ron Sutter—played for Calgary, as did Darryl's son, Brett.

Edmonton Oilers—During the Wayne Gretzky-led dynasty of the 1980s, the Oilers scored at least 400 goals five seasons in a row.

Los Angeles Kings—In 2012 the eighth-seeded Kings beat the New Jersey Devils to win their first Stanley Cup.

San Jose Sharks—The Sharks aren't the first NHL team to play in California's San Francisco Bay area; the Oakland Seals were part of the 1967 expansion class but lasted just nine years.

Vancouver Canucks—The Canucks are still waiting for their first Stanley Cup, but the city of Vancouver isn't; in 1915 a team called the Vancouver Millionaires won the trophy.

TRIVIA

Name the six NHL teams whose nicknames are animals.

Answer: Bruins (a bear), Coyotes, Ducks, Panthers, Penguins, Sharks

CHAMPIONS

Since the late 1800s, hockey teams have competed for the Stanley Cup, which goes to the sport's champion every year. The NHL was created in 1917, and the famous trophy became the ultimate prize for teams in the world's best hockey league. No team captured more Cups than the Montreal Canadiens, who have won it an amazing 24 times, including once before the NHL even existed.

STANLEY CUP CHAMPIONS

TEAM	YEARS WON
Montreal Canadiens	1916, 1924, 1930, 1931, 1944, 1946, 1953, 1956, 1957, 1958, 1959, 1960, 1965, 1966, 1968, 1969, 1971, 1973, 1976, 1977, 1978, 1979, 1986, 1993
Toronto Maple Leafs	1918, 1922, 1932, 1942, 1945, 1947, 1948, 1949, 1951, 1962, 1963, 1964, 1967
Detroit Red Wings	1936, 1937, 1943, 1950, 1952, 1954, 1955, 1997, 1998, 2002, 2008
Boston Bruins	1929, 1939, 1941, 1970, 1972, 2011
Edmonton Oilers	1984, 1985, 1987, 1988, 1990
Chicago Blackhawks	1934, 1938, 1961, 2010, 2013
New York Rangers	1928, 1933, 1940, 1994
New York Islanders	1980, 1981, 1982, 1983

Team	Years	Team	Years
New Jersey Devils	1995, 2000, 2003	Pittsburgh Penguins	1991, 1992, 2009
Colorado Avalanche	1996, 2001	Philadelphia Flyers	1974, 1975
Anaheim Ducks	2007	Calgary Flames	1989
Carolina Hurricanes	2006	Dallas Stars	1999
Los Angeles Kings	2012, 2014	Tampa Bay Lightning	2004

OTHER STANLEY CUP WINNERS—NHL ERA

Ottawa Senators	1921, 1923, 1927	Montreal Maroons	1926, 1935

OTHER STANLEY CUP WINNERS—PRE-NHL

Ottawa Silver Screen	1903*, 1904, 1905, 1906*
Montreal AAA	1893, 1894, 1902*, 1903*
Montreal Victorias	1895, 1896*, 1897, 1898, 1899*
Montreal Wanderers	1906*, 1907*, 1908, 1910

Winnipeg Victorias	1896*, 1901, 1902*	Montreal Shamrocks	1899*, 1900
Ottawa Senators	1909, 1911	Quebec Bulldogs	1912, 1913
Kenora Thistles	1907*	Seattle Metropolitans	1917
Toronto Blueshirts	1914	Vancouver Millionaires	1915

*Years the Stanley Cup was shared by leagues

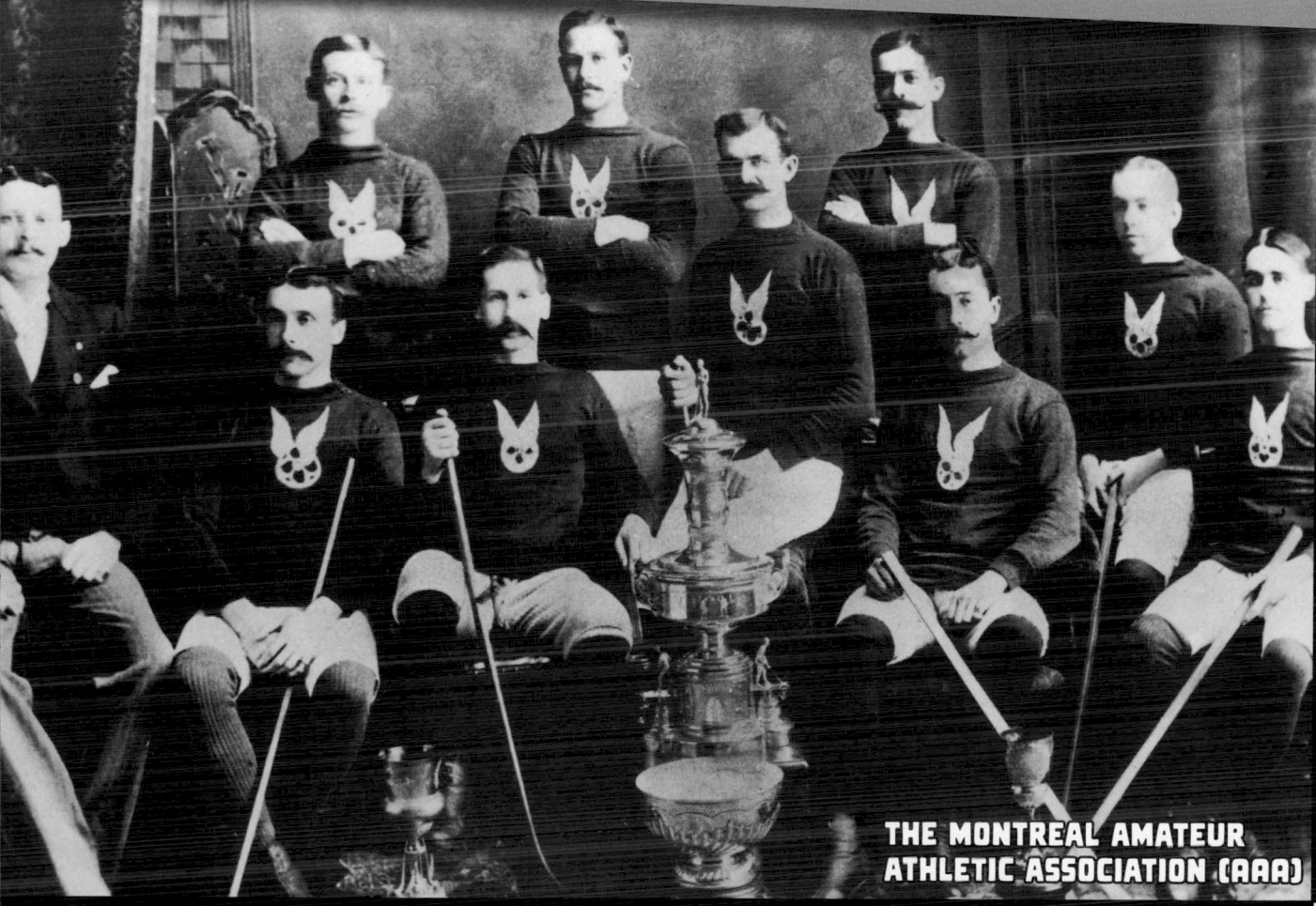

THE MONTREAL AMATEUR ATHLETIC ASSOCIATION (AAA)

DYNASTIES

Every so often a team becomes so good that it dominates for several years in a row. Those eras are known as dynasties. The NHL recognizes nine dynasties throughout its history. Five franchises have made up those dynasties.

BRYAN TROTTIER

NEW YORK ISLANDERS

From 1979 to 1983, the Islanders made NHL history. They became the first franchise from the United States to win four straight Stanley Cups. Their first championship took place eight years after the team was added to the NHL. Seven Hall of Famers, including coach Al Arbour, were part of the historic teams, which had a 16–3 finals record.

TORONTO MAPLE LEAFS

The Maple Leafs captured four Stanley Cups, including three in a row, between 1946 and 1951. Thirteen Hall of Famers, including president Conn Smythe, were part of the Toronto team during that stretch. The Maple Leafs made another great run in the 1960s. They won four more Cups between 1961 and 1967. Sixteen Hall of Famers helped make the second Leafs dynasty possible.

MONTREAL CANADIENS

The Canadiens have won more Stanley Cups than any other team. They also put together three dynasties: 1956–1960, 1964–1969, and 1975–1979. Montreal's first dynasty included five consecutive Cup wins. Twelve players from that era are now in the Hall of Fame. The second dynasty included four more titles and many of the same players. The final dynasty won four Stanley Cups in a row and featured 11 Hall of Famers.

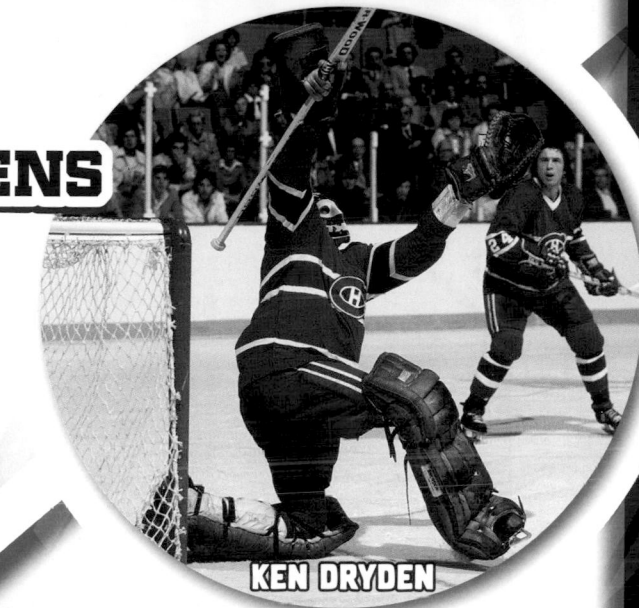

KEN DRYDEN

OTTAWA SENATORS

The Ottawa dynasty rose to power as the original Senators. Between 1919 and 1927, the Senators became the NHL's first dynasty. They won four Stanley Cups behind 14 future Hall of Famers. One of those players, King Clancy, played every position on the ice— including goaltender—during a 1923 Cup finals game.

EDMONTON OILERS

Edmonton Oilers center Wayne Gretzky

Having the great Wayne Gretzky was a big reason why the Oilers were a dynasty from 1983 to 1990. But Edmonton had so much more. In fact, when Edmonton won its fifth championship during the run, Gretzky had already been traded to the Los Angeles Kings. During both the 1983–1984 and the 1985–1986 seasons, the Oilers had three players with 50 goals or more and four players with 100 points or more. Six Hall of Famers led Edmonton on its great run.

GREATEST SEASONS

Each season one team stands tall after a grueling regular season and a hard-fought playoffs. With the Stanley Cup hoisted high, the players skate around the rink as NHL champions. But there are only a few teams that have had truly historic seasons. From star players to masterful coaching, these teams set NHL records that still stand today. It's easy to see why these teams are considered the greatest of all time.

MOST POINTS: 1976-1977 MONTREAL CANADIENS

During their 1970s dynasty, the Montreal Canadiens compiled one of the best seasons in NHL history. In 1976−1977 they went 60−8−12. They ended with a record 132 points for the regular-season standings (two points for wins, one point for ties). Right wing Guy Lafleur scored 56 goals and had 136 points, and Steve Shutt scored 60 goals. The Canadiens scored 216 more goals than their opponents. Montreal cruised through the playoffs, losing just twice and sweeping the Boston Bruins in the finals for its 20th Stanley Cup.

HIGHEST-SCORING TEAM: 1983-1984 EDMONTON OILERS

The 1983–1984 Oilers team was a well-oiled scoring machine. The first year they won a Stanley Cup, they set a scoring record with 446 goals—an average of more than 5.5 goals per game. Wayne Gretzky led the way with 87 goals and 205 points. Glenn Anderson and Jari Kurri scored more than 50 goals each. Kurri, Mark Messier, and defenseman Paul Coffey each had more than 100 points.

MOST WINS: 1995-1996 DETROIT RED WINGS

In 1995–1996 the Detroit Red Wings were dominant during the regular season, winning a record 62 games. They were led by top-scorer Sergei Fedorov, who had 107 points, and longtime captain Steve Yzerman, who had 95 points. Coach Scotty Bowman, who also coached the 1976–1977 Canadiens, was behind the bench. Detroit won the President's Trophy as the team with the best regular-season record. However, their great season was spoiled when they failed to win the Stanley Cup.

BEST WIN PERCENTAGE: 1929-1930 BOSTON BRUINS

In the 1920s and 1930, NHL teams played only 44 games in a season compared to 82 today. In 1929–1930 the Boston Bruins had what still stands as the league's record-best winning percentage. Behind great defenseman Eddie Shore, the team went 38–5–1 for a .875 success rate. Although the Bruins won the Stanley Cup a year earlier, they were unable to repeat in 1929–1930.

COACHES

They are known as the bench bosses, the ringmasters, and the geniuses behind the game. Coaches have the task of putting the right line combinations together, selecting the best goalies, and motivating their teams to play to their full potential.

SCOTTY BOWMAN

Scotty Bowman deserves a spot at the top of the list of greatest hockey coaches. He coached for 30 seasons and won 1,244 games—462 more victories than Al Arbour, the second coach on the list. Bowman won nine Stanley Cup championships—five with the Canadiens, three with the Red Wings, and one with the Penguins. Bowman won his first Stanley Cup in 1973 and his last in 2002.

AL ARBOUR

It didn't take long for the New York Islanders to go from an expansion team to an NHL dynasty. Coach Al Arbour is a big reason why. The coach took over the team in 1973, one year after the Islanders were created. By the end of the 1979–1980 season, they were Stanley Cup champions. New York also won the next three Cups behind Arbour. In 23 seasons Arbour compiled 782 wins, good enough for second on the all-time wins list.

HERB BROOKS

One of the great coaching jobs of all time didn't take place in the NHL. Although Herb Brooks coached in the NHL for seven seasons and had only two losing seasons, his triumphant moment came during the 1980 Olympics. He led Team USA to the greatest upset in sports history. During the "Miracle on Ice" the Americans defeated the mighty Soviet Union team in Lake Placid, New York. A master motivator, Brooks also won three college titles at the University of Minnesota.

Top Coaches

- Jack Adams, Red Wings/Cougars/Falcons—coach of the year trophy is named after the three-time Cup winner
- Al Arbour, Blues/Islanders—led Isles dynasty that won four championships in a row
- Mike Babcock, Ducks/Red Wings—Only coach to win a Stanley Cup, an Olympic gold medal, and a world championship.
- Toe Blake, Canadiens—won eight Cups with Montreal, including five in a row
- Scotty Bowman, Blues/Canadiens/Sabres/Penguins/Red Wings—won nine Stanley Cups, more than any other coach
- Hap Day, Maple Leafs—led Toronto to five Cup victories
- Punch Imlach, Maple Leafs/Sabres—oversaw the Leafs' second dynasty, winning four titles
- Dick Irvin, Blackhawks/Maple Leafs/Canadiens—won four Stanley Cups
- Mike Keenan, Flyers/Blackhawks/Rangers/Blues/Canucks/Bruins/Panthers/Flames—ranks fifth in all-time wins
- Glen Sather, Oilers/Rangers—won four championships with Edmonton dynasty

MIKE KEENAN

CHAPTER 7

PLAYOFF RECORDS

In the NHL every team starts the season aiming to make the playoffs. The ultimate prize is making it to the Stanley Cup finals and winning a championship. The postseason has featured many outstanding, memorable performances. Some of those performances have put players and teams into the record books. When a record leads to a championship, it's that much sweeter.

Tampa Bay Lightning forward Brad Richards won the Conn Smythe trophy in 2004 as the most valuable player of the playoffs— and for good reason. Not only did he lead the Lightning to its first Stanley Cup title, but he set an NHL record by scoring seven game-winning goals along the way.

If you ever wondered how good goaltender Patrick Roy was, look no further than his playoff records. No goalie in NHL history has played in more playoff games. His total of 247 appearances puts him third all-time among all players.

▼ **Boston Bruins**

MOST CHAMPIONSHIPS		
1.	Montreal Canadiens	23
2.	Toronto Maple Leafs	13
3.	Detroit Red Wings	11
4.	Boston Bruins	6
5.	Edmonton Oilers	5
	Chicago Blackhawks	5
7	New York Islanders	4
	New York Rangers	4
9.	New Jersey Devils	3
	Pittsburgh Penguins	3

▼ Montreal Canadiens

REPEAT CHAMPIONS

The Montreal Canadiens are the only team to win five consecutive championships, winning the Stanley Cup each year from 1956 through 1960. The Canadiens also won four in a row from 1976 through 1979. The only other team to win four in a row was the New York Islanders, champions from 1980 through 1983.

▲ New York Islanders

RECORD FACT The New York Islanders hold the record for consecutive playoff series wins. Between 1980 and 1984, they won 19 series in a row, including four Stanley Cups. They finally lost to the Edmonton Oilers in the 1984 Cup finals.

CLUTCH SCORERS

Five players have scored five goals in a single playoff game.

Newsy Lalonde	Montreal Canadiens	1919
Maurice Richard	Montreal Canadiens	1944
Darryl Sittler	Toronto Maple Leafs	1976
Reggie Leach	Philadelphia Flyers	1976
Mario Lemieux	Pittsburgh Penguins	1989

▲ **Maurice Richard**

PLAYOFF POWER-PLAY GOALS (SINGLE SEASON)

1.	**Mike Bossy**	9	Islanders	1981
	Cam Neely	9	Bruins	1991
3.	**John Druce**	8	Capitals	1990
	Tim Kerr	8	Flyers	1989
	Mario Lemieux	8	Penguins	1992
	Brian Propp	8	North Stars	1991
7.	**Several players tied with**	7		

▲ **Mario Lemieux**

RECORD FACT Six players have scored three short-handed goals during a playoff run. Naturally, Wayne Gretzky was one of them, accomplishing the feat in 1983. Bill Barber, Lorne Henning, Todd Marchant, Wayne Presley, and Derek Sanderson complete the list.

▼ Dustin Byfuglien

PLAYOFF GAME-WINNING GOALS (SINGLE SEASON) ||||||

1.	Brad Richards	7	Lightning	2004
2.	Joe Nieuwendyk	6	Stars	1999
	Joe Sakic	6	Avalanche	1996
4.	Mike Bossy	5	Islanders	1983
	Dustin Byfuglien	5	Blackhawks	2010
	Johan Franzen	5	Red Wings	2008
	Jari Kurri	5	Oilers	1987
	Mario Lemieux	5	Penguins	1992
	Fernando Pisani	5	Oilers	2006
	Bobby Smith	5	North Stars	1991

RECORD FACT Wayne Gretzky and Brett Hull have scored more game-winning playoff goals than any other players. Each netted 24 winners in his career. Joe Sakic has the record for overtime game-winners, scoring eight in his playoff career.

OVERTIME WINNERS

Sixteen players in NHL history have scored a goal in overtime that gave their team the Stanley Cup championship. In 2014, the Los Angeles Kings' Alec Martinez scored with 5:17 remaining in the second overtime to clinch the cup against the New York Rangers. Two players, Brett Hull of the Dallas Stars in 1999 and Uwe Krupp of the Colorado Avalanche in 1996, won the Cup with a goal in triple overtime. Only two finals have gone beyond the distance, going into overtime in Game 7. The Detroit Red Wings won both of those games, with Pete Babando scoring in double overtime in 1950 and Tony Leswick scoring in overtime for the 1954 championship.

▲ Patrick Kane

1.	Chris Chelios	266	Canadiens/Blackhawks/Red Wings	24 playoffs
2.	Nicklas Lidstrom	263	Red Wings	20 playoffs
3.	Patrick Roy	247	Canadiens/Avalanche	17 playoffs
4.	Mark Messier	236	Oilers/Rangers/Canucks	17 playoffs
5.	Claude Lemieux	234	Canadiens/Devils/Avalanche/Coyotes/Stars/Sharks	18 playoffs
6.	Scott Stevens	233	Capitals/Blues/Devils	20 playoffs
7.	Guy Carbonneau	231	Canadiens/Blues/Stars	17 playoffs
8.	Larry Robinson	227	Canadiens/Kings	20 playoffs
9.	Glenn Anderson	225	Oilers/Maple Leafs/Rangers/Blues	15 playoffs
10.	Kris Draper	222	Jets/Red Wings	18 playoffs

1.	Patrick Roy	247	Canadiens/Avalanche	17 playoffs
2.	Martin Brodeur	205	Devils	17 playoffs*
3.	Ed Belfour	161	Blackhawks/Stars/Maple Leafs	13 playoffs
4.	Grant Fuhr	150	Oilers/Sabres/Blues	14 playoffs
5.	Mike Vernon	138	Flames/Red Wings/Sharks/Panthers	14 playoffs
6.	Curtis Joseph	133	Blues/Oilers/Maple Leafs/Red Wings/Flames	14 playoffs
7.	Andy Moog	132	Oilers/Bruins/Stars/Canadiens	16 playoffs
	Billy Smith	132	Kings/Islanders	13 playoffs
9.	Chris Osgood	129	Red Wings/Islanders/Blues	13 playoffs
10.	Tom Barrasso	119	Sabres/Penguins/Senators	13 playoffs
	Dominik Hasek	119	Blackhawks/Sabres/Red Wings	13 playoffs

*Active player

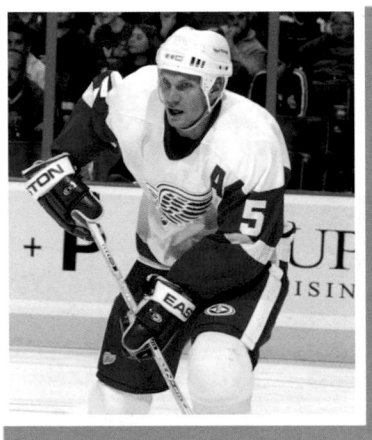

▲ Nicklas Lidstrom

GOALIE PLAYOFF WINS (CAREER) |||||||||||||||||||||||||||

1.	Patrick Roy	151	Canadiens/Avalanche	17 playoffs
2	Martin Brodeur	113	Devils	17 playoffs*
3.	Grant Fuhr	92	Oilers/Sabres/Blues	14 playoffs
4.	Ed Belfour	88	Blackhawks/Stars/Maple Leafs	13 playoffs
	Billy Smith	88	Kings/Islanders	13 playoffs
6.	Ken Dryden	80	Canadiens	8 playoffs
7.	Mike Vernon	77	Flames/Red Wings/Sharks/Panthers	14 playoffs
8.	Chris Osgood	74	Red Wings/Islanders/Blues	13 playoffs
9.	Jacques Plante	71	Canadiens	16 playoffs
10.	Andy Moog	68	Oilers/Bruins/Stars/Canadiens	16 playoffs

*Active player

THE STANLEY CUP

The oldest and most famous trophy in professional sports in North America is the Stanley Cup. It goes to the NHL champion each year. One of the things that makes the Cup special is that each member of the winning team gets his name engraved on it. The name of Henri Richard of the Montreal Canadiens is etched into the silver trophy 11 times—more than any other player. But Jean Beliveau of the Canadiens has his name on it more than any other person. It's on there 10 times as a player and another seven as a member of the team's management. Another layer is added to the cup when there's no more space to add names.

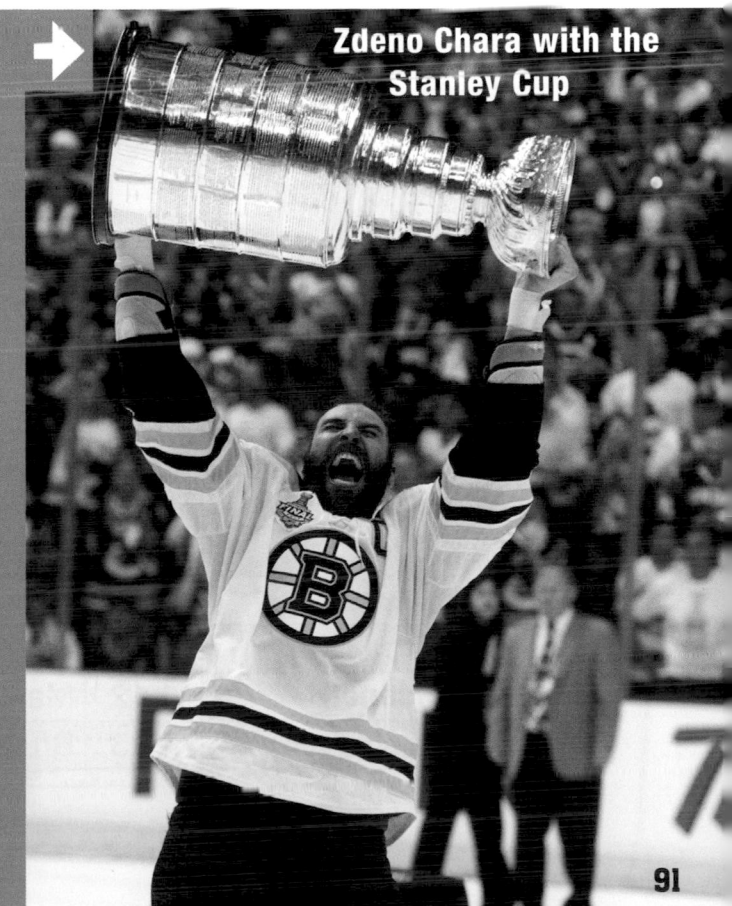

Zdeno Chara with the Stanley Cup

PLAYOFF SHUTOUTS

CAREER

1.	**Martin Brodeur**	24	Devils	17 playoffs*
2.	**Patrick Roy**	23	Canadiens/Avalanche	17 playoffs
3.	**Curtis Joseph**	16	Blues/Oilers/Maple Leafs/Red Wings/Flames	14 playoffs
4.	**Chris Osgood**	15	Red Wings/Islanders/Blues	13 playoffs
5.	**Jacques Plante**	14	Canadiens/Blues/Maple Leafs/Bruins	16 playoffs
	Dominik Hasek	14	Blackhawks/Sabres/Red Wings	13 playoffs
	Ed Belfour	14	Blackhawks/Stars/Maple Leafs	13 playoffs
8.	**Turk Broda**	13	Maple Leafs	13 playoffs
9.	**Terry Sawchuk**	12	Red Wings/Maple Leafs/Kings/Rangers	15 playoffs
10.	**Ken Dryden**	10	Canadiens	8 playoffs

*Active player

HIGHEST-SCORING GAMES

The Los Angeles Kings defeated the Edmonton Oilers 10-8 on April 7, 1982. The 18 goals were the most scored by two teams in a playoff game. In 1989 the Pittsburgh Penguins defeated the Philadelphia Flyers 10-7. The most goals scored by one team in a playoff game is 13, racked up by the Oilers in a 13-3 win over the Kings April 9, 1987.

▼ Marcel Dionne of the Los Angeles Kings

PLAYOFF SHUTOUTS

SINGLE SEASON				
1.	Martin Brodeur	7	Devils	2003
2.	Dominik Hasek	6	Red Wings	2002
3.	Miikka Kiprusoff	5	Flames	2004
	Nikolai Khabibulin	5	Lightning	2004
	Jean-Sebastien Giguere	5	Ducks	2003
6.	Many players tied with	4		

▼ Nikolai Khabibulin

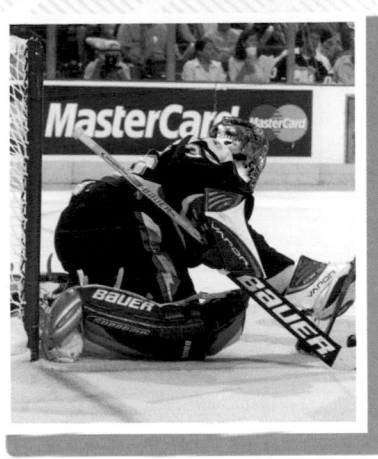

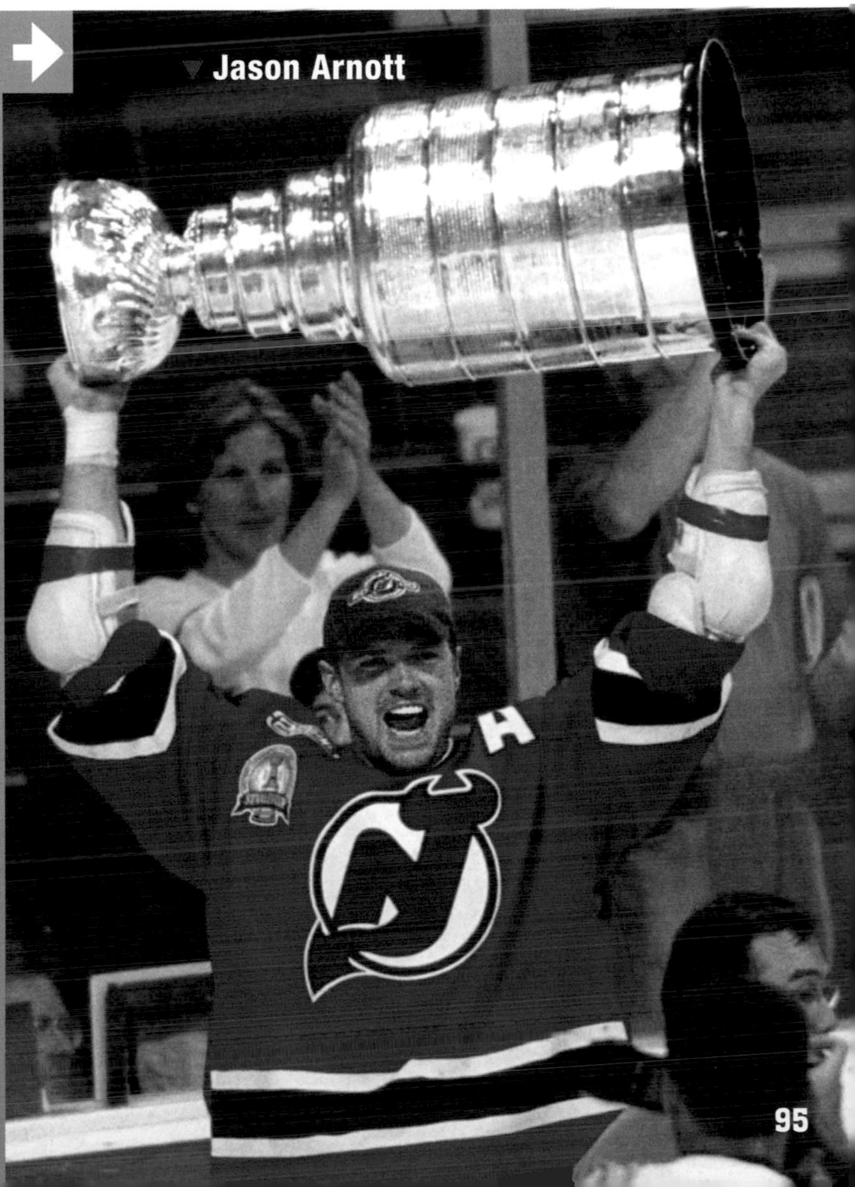

▼ Jason Arnott

PLAYING TILL THE END

One of the most exciting things about playoff hockey is the fact that there are no ties or shootouts. Overtime games are played until a goal is scored. For the game's two goalies, all of the pressure is on them. In Stanley Cup playoff history, Ed Belfour has won more overtime games than any other goaltender. His 20 overtime wins include a triple-overtime victory in Game 6 of the 1999 finals that clinched the Stanley Cup. A year later, though, he gave up the Cup-winning goal to Jason Arnott of the New Jersey Devils.

CHAPTER 8

FAN FAVORITES

ARENAS

OUT WITH THE OLD

The NHL's Original Six teams—the Canadiens, Maple Leafs, Bruins, Blackhawks, Red Wings, and Rangers—played in magnificent old buildings for most of their history. Those arenas included the Montreal Forum, Maple Leaf Gardens, Boston Garden, Chicago Stadium, the Detroit Olympia Stadium, and an older version of Madison Square Garden. The teams have since moved from those old "barns" and into state-of-the-art arenas. One of the oldest arenas in the NHL is Nassau Veterans Memorial Coliseum, home to the Islanders since 1972.

DETROIT RED WINGS' JOE LOUIS ARENA

MINNESOTA WILD'S XCEL ENERGY CENTER

IN WITH THE NEW

Many new arenas have been built for NHL teams in recent years. The newest building is the Penguins' Consol Energy Center, which the team moved into in 2010. Many surveys have named the Minnesota Wild's Xcel Energy Center as the best building in the league for both fans and players—of all ages. Besides being home to the self-proclaimed State of Hockey's professional team, it is also home to a college hockey championship and the boys and girls high school state championships.

SIT IN THE SADDLE

One of the most unique NHL arenas is the Flames' Scotiabank Saddledome. Why is it called the Saddledome? Because it looks like a giant could straddle the building and ride it across western Canada. Like a saddle atop a horse, the building has a low middle and high ends. The Saddledome was the site of Olympic hockey and figure skating in 1988, and the Flames played in three Stanley Cup Finals series there.

ON FROZEN POND

Each year the NHL honors hockey's outdoor beginnings by playing a New Year's Day game outside in the cold—and sometimes the snow. The NHL Winter Classic isn't played on lakes or rivers, though. A rink is set up in an outdoor stadium. The first was played in 2008 in Buffalo's Ralph Wilson Stadium. Then it went to a pair of historic baseball stadiums: Chicago's Wrigley Field in 2009 and Boston's Fenway Park in 2010.

WRIGLEY FIELD, 2009 NHL WINTER CLASSIC

Five Largest Hockey Arenas

1. Bell Centre (Canadiens)	21,273
2. Joe Louis Arena (Red Wings)	20,066
3. United Center (Blackhawks)	19,717
4. Wells Fargo Center (Flyers)	19,519
5. Tampa Bay Times Forum (Lightning)	19,500

NHL TROPHIES

The NHL is known for its trophies, which it hands out to its best players every season. The Hart Trophy has been given out to the league MVP since 1924, and the Conn Smythe Trophy has gone to the best player in the playoffs since 1965.

STANLEY CUP

No trophy in hockey—perhaps in any sport—is as famous as the Stanley Cup. The Cup is awarded to the team that wins the NHL playoff championship every season. The oldest trophy in professional sports, the Cup was first donated to hockey in 1892 by Sir Frederick Arthur Stanley, known as Lord Stanley of Preston. When a team wins the Cup, each player's name is engraved on the silver trophy, and each player gets to take it home for one day in the offseason.

STANLEY CUP FACTS

- The Canadiens' Henri Richard had his name engraved on the Cup a record 11 times as a player.

- Jean Beliveau has his name on the Cup 17 times as both a player and coach.

- Scotty Bowman won the Cup a record nine times as a coach.

- The first team to engrave its roster on the Cup was the Montreal Wanderers in 1907.

- The Cup is 35 ¼ inches (90 cm) high and weighs 34 ½ pounds (15.6 kg). It continues to grow because sections are added to fit the names of the new champions.

NHL AWARD TROPHIES

Art Ross Trophy
leading point scorer

Bill Masterton Memorial Trophy
player who displays perseverance and dedication to hockey

Calder Memorial Trophy
rookie of the year

Conn Smythe Trophy
most valuable player of the playoffs

Cam Ward with the 2006 Conn Smythe Trophy

Frank J. Selke Trophy
top defensive forward

Hart Memorial Trophy
most valuable player

Jack Adams Award
coach of the year

James Norris Memorial Trophy
top defenseman

King Clancy Memorial Trophy
player who displays leadership on the ice and in the community

Lady Byng Memorial Trophy
player who displays gentlemanly conduct

Maurice "Rocket" Richard Trophy
leading goal scorer

Ted Lindsay Award
MVP as voted on by the players

Vezina Trophy
top goaltender

William M. Jennings Trophy
goaltender with the lowest goals-against average

GREAT NICKNAMES

From "Mr. Hockey" Gordie Howe and "The Great One" Wayne Gretzky to Sid "The Kid" Crosby, hockey players are known for their nicknames. Rarely do players get called by their birth names when they're on the rink. Some nicknames have stuck throughout NHL history.

SID "THE KID" CROSBY

"THE GOLDEN JET" BOBBY HULL

In an era before helmets, Bobby Hull was known for his fast skating and his flowing blond hair.

BERNIE "BOOM BOOM" GEOFFRION

The Canadiens star of the 1950s got his great nickname from the sound that is made by the shot he supposedly invented—the slap shot.

MAURICE "ROCKET" RICHARD

The Canadiens' star was known for his intensity and speed, skating like a rocket around the Montreal Forum. He went to the All-Star Game 13 times and entered the NHL Hall of Fame in 1961.

"MR. ZERO" FRANK BRIMSEK

As a goalie with the Bruins in 1939–1940, Frank Brimsek earned his nickname by recording 10 shutouts and a pair of amazing scoreless streaks. One streak lasted 231 minutes, 54 seconds, and another spanned 220 minutes, 24 seconds en route to a Stanley Cup. He had 40 shutouts in his 10-year career.

DAVE "THE HAMMER" SCHULTZ

One of the great fighters in NHL history, Dave Schultz was one of the Flyers' famed "Broad Street Bullies." He led the NHL in penalty minutes four times during his career.

TRIVIA

Can you match these 10 nicknames to the correct player?

1. The Wrecking Ball		Al Arbour
2. The Red Baron		Gordon Berenson
3. The Monster		Derek Boogard
4. The Russian Rocket		Adam Brown
5. The Flying Scotsman		Pavel Bure
6. Radar		Johan Franzen
7. The Finnish Flash		Jonas Gustavsson
8. Cyclone		Mark Recchi
9. The Boogie Man		Teemu Selanne
10. The Mule		Marvin Wentworth

Answer: 1. Mark Recchi 2. Gordon Berenson 3. Jonas Gustavsson 4. Pavel Bure 5. Adam Brown 6. Al Arbour 7. Teemu Selanne 8. Marvin Wentworth 9. Derek Boogaard 10. Johan Franzon

OUTSIDE THE NHL

OLYMPIC HOCKEY

The NHL isn't the only place to showcase the great game of hockey. Some of the most exciting moments on the ice have taken place during the Winter Olympics.

The United States men's hockey team has won two gold medals, one in 1960 and one in 1980. In 1980 the young U.S. team pulled off the "Miracle on Ice." Behind the heroics of captain Mike Eruzione and goalie Jim Craig, the U.S. upset the favored Soviet Union 4-3. Eruzione scored the game-winning goal, and Craig made 39 saves. Two days later the Americans defeated Finland 4-2 for the gold medal.

In 2010 in Vancouver, British Columbia, Canada, the United States men played in one of the most memorable Olympic hockey games. In the early rounds of the Olympic tournament, the Americans upset the Canadians 5-3. In a final-game rematch Canada took an early lead and held it for most of the game. The game headed to overtime after U.S. forward Zach Parise tied the game with 25 seconds left in regulation. Penguins star Sidney Crosby gave the Canadians the gold medal with a thrilling goal in sudden-death overtime. Canada won Olympic gold again in 2014 in Sochi, Russia.

USA'S 1980 OLYMPIC HOCKEY TEAM

CANADA'S 2010 MEN'S OLYMPIC HOCKEY TEAM

WOMEN'S HOCKEY

Women and girls play at many levels: youth, high school, college, and international play. The NHL has expressed interest in creating a professional hockey league for women as well. Women's hockey has been an Olympic sport since 1998, when the United States won the gold medal in Nagano, Japan. Canada has won the last four gold medals, with the U.S. taking silver in 2002, 2010 and 2014. In Sochi, Russia, Canada made a stunning third-period comeback and won gold on Marie-Philip Poulin's goal in overtime.

Women's Canadian gold medal hockey team, 2010

COLLEGE HOCKEY

A popular level of hockey in the United States is the college game. The game is played mostly in the West, Midwest, and the Northeast. Some NHL stars who have won the Hobey Baker Award as college hockey's best player include Neal Broten (Minnesota, 1981), Paul Kariya (Maine, 1993), Chris Drury (Boston University, 1998), and Ryan Miller (Michigan State, 2001).

Boston College versus University of Wisconsin, 2010 NCAA Men's National Championship

RECENT NCAA DIVISION 1 WINNERS

Men's		Women's	
2014	Union Dutchmen	2014	Clarkson Golden Knights
2013	Yale Bulldogs	2013	Minnesota Golden Gophers
2012	Boston College Eagles	2012	Minnesota Golden Gophers
2011	Minnesota-Duluth Bulldogs	2011	Wisconsin Badgers
2010	Boston College Eagles	2010	Minnesota-Duluth Bulldogs
2009	Boston University Terriers	2009	Wisconsin Badgers

AROUND THE NHL

MASKED MEN

Goalies are some of the game's most interesting characters. One place where they show off their personality is on their protective masks. Many of the masks have detailed pictures painted on the helmets. The Buffalo Sabres' Ryan Miller's helmet features the head of a red-eyed, blue-and-yellow buffalo. Former New York Rangers goalie Mike Richter had the head of the Statue of Liberty on his mask. Two fearsome skeletons creep along the helmet of Evgeni Nabokov of the San Jose Sharks.

CHRIS MASON

EVGENI NABOKOV

BREAKING BARRIERS

On January 18, 1958, history was made when Bruins winger Willie O'Ree took the ice. O'Ree was the first black player to participate in an NHL game. The Canada native had a short professional career. He played in just two games that season and 43 games in 1960–1961 when he scored four goals. In 1992 the Lightning made history when they signed goaltender Manon Rheaume to a contract. She was the first and only woman to play in the NHL. Her only NHL playing time came during an exhibition game, but she also had a short minor-league career.

A REAL DREAM TEAM

In 1987 Canada put together one of the finest hockey teams ever assembled to compete for the Canada Cup. Long before NHL players were allowed to skate in the Olympics, the Canada Cup was an international tournament featuring pro players. Imagine a team with Mario Lemieux passing to Wayne Gretzky and back to Lemieux for a goal. Canada also had Mark Messier at forward, Paul Coffey on defense, and Grant Fuhr in front of the net. "For me," Gretzky said, "it was probably the best hockey I've ever played."

ROLLER HOCKEY

You don't need ice to play hockey. It can be played on wheels too. Some people play roller hockey outdoors in the summer. Others play indoors on specially made roller-skating surfaces. There is even a professional inline-skate league called Major League Roller Hockey. The league has teams in Chicago, Philadelphia, Washington, and other cities. Nashville Predators forward Joel Ward played roller hockey before working his way to the NHL.

MASCOTS

Hockey mascots add even more entertainment to an already exciting sport. They liven up the crowd with loud, energetic cheers. They provide comic relief by humorously falling over or pulling pranks on the refs or members of the other team. Some mascots, such as Al the Octopus, were created by traditions.

These playful creatures are sometimes known as the faces of the franchises, and they are definitely parts of their teams.

FACT:

Four NHL teams have never had a mascot: the Dallas Stars, Edmonton Oilers, New York Rangers, and Philadelphia Flyers.

S.J. SHARKIE OF THE SAN JOSE SHARKS

HARVEY THE HOUND

The first mascot to patrol the stands of an NHL game was the Calgary Flames' dog, Harvey the Hound. Harvey is 6 feet 6 inches (198 cm), weighs 200 pounds (91 kg), and has a long, red tongue hanging from his open mouth. Although mascots usually don't talk, Harvey's tongue has gotten him into some trouble. During a game against the Edmonton Oilers, he started taunting the opposing players from behind the glass. Frustrated Oilers coach Craig MacTavish reached up and ripped the tongue out of the dog's mouth, tossing it into the crowd.

ICEBURGH

Pittsburgh's mascot, a giant Penguin named Iceburgh, is known for making fans smile both during games and outside the arena. The beloved penguin is also a movie star. In 1995 he appeared in the action movie *Sudden Death* with Jean Claude Van Damme.

NORDY

When the Minnesota Wild unveiled its logo in 2000, no one knew what it was. A bear? A cougar? A wolf? Seven years later, the Wild's mascot, Nordy, skated onto the ice for the first time. But the costume didn't clear anything up. All you can say is that he is a wild animal from the north woods with a green "M" on his forehead. He also has a golden mullet—otherwise known as hockey hair—flowing off the back of his neck.

AL THE OCTOPUS

One of the slimiest hockey playoff traditions started in 1952. That's when an octopus was first thrown onto the ice during a Red Wings home playoff game in Detroit. The creature's eight legs represented the eight post-season wins a team needed to capture the Stanley Cup. Although more games are now needed to win the Cup, the tradition continues, and fans still find ways to toss octopuses on the ice. The sea creature is now the Red Wings' unofficial mascot. A giant, inflated purple octopus named Al hangs from the rafters of Joe Louis Arena.

CHAPTER 9

GREATEST MOMENTS

LUCKY NUMBER 7

There are few sporting events as thrilling as a Game 7 of the Stanley Cup Finals. There have been 16 times in NHL history where the championship was decided in Game 7. The latest occurred in 2011, when the Boston Bruins' Patrice Bergeron and Brad Marchand each scored two goals in a shutout of the Vancouver Canucks.

2009 PITTSBURGH PENGUINS

2011 | Bruins 4 | Canucks 0
Goalie Tim Thomas stopped all 37 shots on goal

2009 | Penguins 2 | Red Wings 1
Maxime Talbot scored two goals for Pittsburgh

2006 | Hurricanes 3 | Oilers 1
Rookie goalie Cam Ward won the Conn Smythe Trophy

2004 | Lightning 2 | Flames 1
Ruslan Fedotenko scored both Tampa Bay goals

2003 | Devils 3 | Ducks 0
Goalie Martin Brodeur stopped all 24 shots he faced

2001 | Avalanche 3 | Devils 1
Defenseman Ray Bourque finally won a Cup

2004 TAMPA BAY LIGHTNING

1994
Rangers 3   Canucks 2

Mark Messier helped New York end a 54-year title drought

1987
Oilers 3   Flyers 1

Part of Edmonton's dynasty

1971
Canadiens 3   Blackhawks 2

Rookie goalie Ken Dryden was the playoff MVP

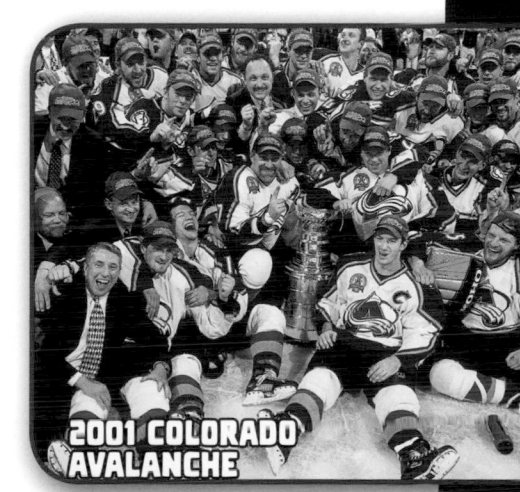

2006 CAROLINA HURRICANES

1965
Canadiens 4   Blackhawks 0

Gump Worsley made 20 saves to shut out Chicago

1964
Maple Leafs 4   Red Wings 0

Johnny Bower made 33 saves in the shutout

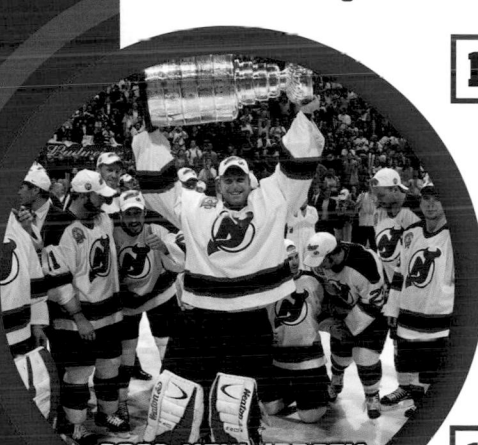

2003 NEW JERSEY DEVILS

1955
Red Wings 3   Canadiens 1

Alex Delvecchio scored two goals for the winners

1954
Red Wings 2   Canadiens 1   OT

The second and most recent Game 7 to go to overtime

1950
Red Wings 4   Rangers 3   2 OT

The first Game 7 to go to overtime

1945
Maple Leafs 2   Red Wings 1

Defenseman Babe Pratt scored the game-winning goal

1942
Maple Leafs 3   Red Wings 1

Toronto erased a 3-games-to-0 deficit in the series

2001 COLORADO AVALANCHE

LONGEST GAMES

One of the reasons playoff hockey games are so exciting is the chance for extended overtime. During the regular season, there is only one overtime before the teams have a shootout. In a shootout, each team has five chances for one of its players to shoot a goal one-on-one with the goalie. The team with the most goals in the shootout wins.

After the regular season ends, shootouts are no longer used to decide a winner. Instead, the games continue until a goal is scored—sudden death. But sometimes the end of the game isn't so sudden. Twice, games have gone into a sixth overtime before someone scores the deciding goal. That's almost the length of two more full games!

WORTH THE WAIT

The longest Stanley Cup-clinching game took place in 1999 when the Dallas Stars beat the Buffalo Sabres 2-1. Brett Hull beat goalie Dominik Hasek with the rebound goal, which came with 5 minutes, 9 seconds remaining in the third overtime.

Date	Score	Game Time	Winning Goal
March 24, 1936	Red Wings 1, Maroons 0	2:56:30	Mud Bruneteau
April 3, 1933	Maple Leafs 1, Bruins 0	2:44:46	Ken Doraty
May 4, 2000	Flyers 2, Penguins 1	2:32:01	Keith Primeau
April 24, 2003	Ducks 4, Stars 3	2:20:48	Petr Sykora
April 24, 1996	Penguins 3, Capitals 2	2:19:15	Petr Nedved
April 11, 2007	Canucks 5, Stars 4	2:18:06	Henrik Sedin
March 23, 1943	Maple Leafs 3, Red Wings 2	2:10:18	Jack McLean
May 4, 2008	Stars 2, Sharks 1	2:09:03	Brenden Morrow
March 28, 1930	Canadiens 2, Rangers 1	2:08:52	Gus Rivers
April 18, 1987	Islanders 3, Capitals 2	2:08:47	Pat LaFontaine

Note: A regular game has 1:00:00 of playing time

Joe Thornton fights for the puck during the May 4, 2008, matchup against the Stars.

GREATEST GOALS

Great plays are made all over the rink during a hockey game. There are incredible saves, pretty passes, and bone-crushing hits. But some of the greatest plays of all are the awe-inspiring goals.

HEXTALL SHOOTS ... AND SCORES?

Philadelphia Flyers goaltender Ron Hextall did a lot more than stop pucks. He was considered one of the best puck-handling and passing goalies in the league. On December 8, 1987, Hextall did something no other goaltender had ever done before—shoot and score a goal. It happened late in the game after the Bruins had pulled their goalie for an extra skater. Hextall stopped the puck and fired it the length of the ice. It was a bull's-eye, right into the empty net. Only nine other goaltenders have scored or been credited with goals in NHL history.

FACT:

In 1979 the New York Islanders' Billy Smith became the first goalie to be credited with a goal. The score happened after the puck bounced off his chest pad and was accidentally shot in the other net by an opposing player. Smith got the credit because he was the last person on his team to touch the puck before it went into the net.

ORR TAKES FLIGHT

Bobby Orr was a defenseman who wasn't afraid to leave the blue line and get in front of the net. It's what made him one of the greatest players of all time. During the 1970 Stanley Cup Finals, Orr won the championship for the Boston Bruins with one of the greatest overtime goals. Orr passed to teammate Derek Sanderson, who was behind the St. Louis Blues' net. Orr then skated down the goal line toward the net. He got the puck back from Sanderson and tapped it into the net before being tripped and flying through the air in celebration.

"THE GOAL"

Alex Ovechkin wasn't in the league long before he had a highlight reel that would make veteran players jealous. During his rookie season, he scored what Washington Capitals fans simply refer to as "the goal." After racing down the ice on a rush, Ovechkin appeared to be checked to the ice. He fell to the ice with his back to the goal and his hands above his head. Somehow the future superstar still found a way to shoot the puck past the goalie and into the net.

A LEGG UP

Great goals aren't just scored in the NHL. College players have made jaws drop too. In 1996 University of Michigan forward Mike Legg was alone with the puck behind the University of Minnesota net. He picked up the puck with his stick and tucked it into the upper corner of the goal. It looked more like a lacrosse goal than a hockey goal. The Wolverines went on to beat the Gophers in the NCAA tournament game.

WHICH WAY DID HE GO?

In 2008 Columbus Blue Jackets star forward Rick Nash secured a spot on the list of all-time great goals. He carried the puck into the attacking zone where two defensemen were preparing to stop him. He faked out one defenseman, then another, and then faked out the Coyotes' goaltender before scoring. The goal has been watched on YouTube more than 1 million times.

RINK RECORDS

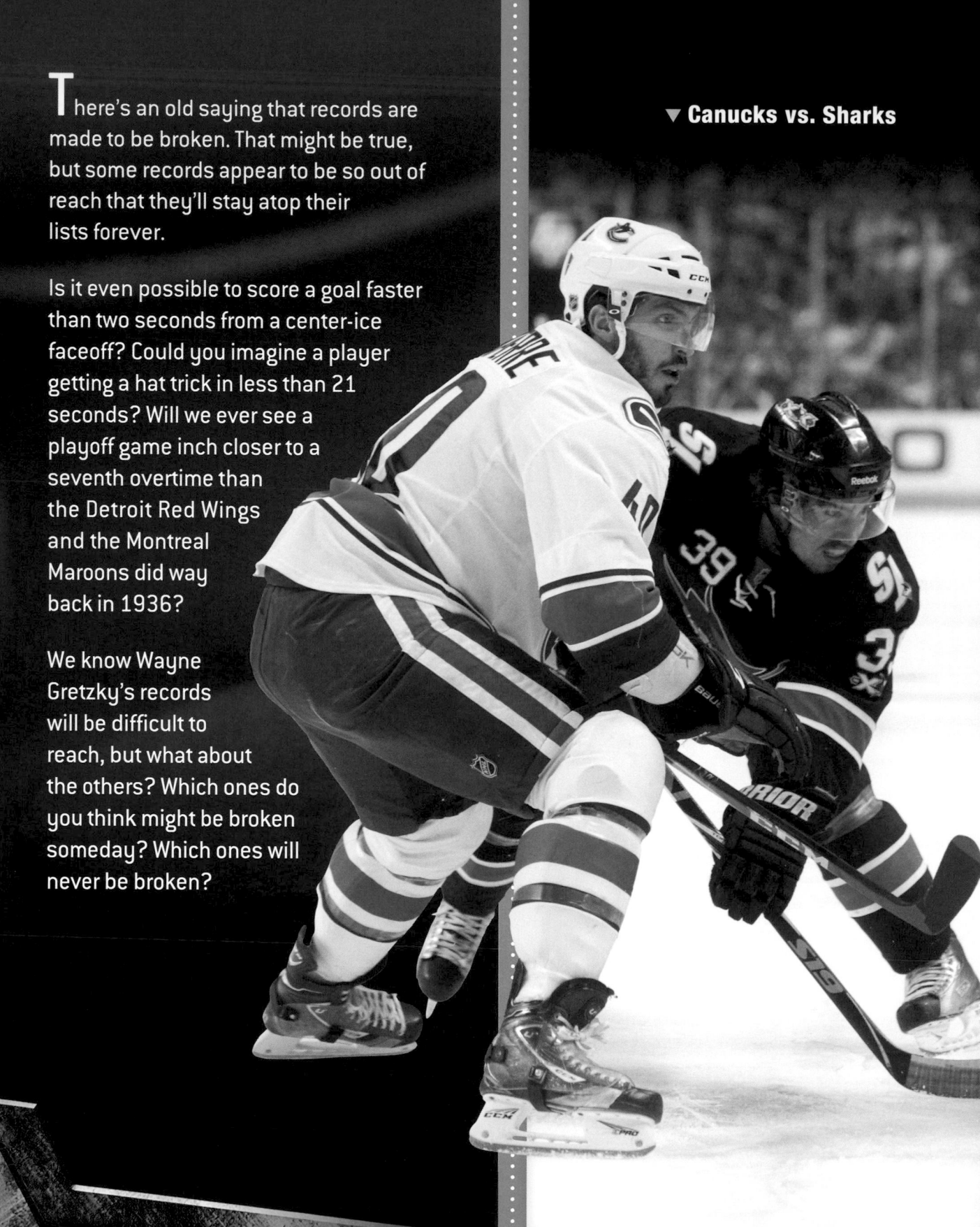

There's an old saying that records are made to be broken. That might be true, but some records appear to be so out of reach that they'll stay atop their lists forever.

Is it even possible to score a goal faster than two seconds from a center-ice faceoff? Could you imagine a player getting a hat trick in less than 21 seconds? Will we ever see a playoff game inch closer to a seventh overtime than the Detroit Red Wings and the Montreal Maroons did way back in 1936?

We know Wayne Gretzky's records will be difficult to reach, but what about the others? Which ones do you think might be broken someday? Which ones will never be broken?

▼ Canucks vs. Sharks

▼ Bryan Trottier

FASTEST GOALS TO START A GAME

1.	Doug Smail	5 seconds	Jets	1981
	Bryan Trottier	5 seconds	Islanders	1984
	Alexander Mogilny	5 seconds	Sabres	1991
4.	Henry Boucha	6 seconds	Red Wings	1973
	Jean Pronovost	6 seconds	Penguins	1976
	Alex Burrows	6 seconds	Canucks	2013
6.	Charlie Conacher	7 seconds	Maple Leafs	1932
	Danny Gare	7 seconds	Sabres	1978
	Tiger Williams	7 seconds	Kings	1987
	Evgeni Malkin	7 seconds	Penguins	2011

LONGEST GAMES

1.	Red Wings 1, Maroons 0	2:56:30	March 24, 1936
2.	Maple Leafs 1, Bruins 0	2:44:46	April 3, 1933
3.	Flyers 2, Penguins 1	2:32:01	May 4, 2000
4.	Ducks 4, Stars 3	2:20:48	April 24, 2003
5.	Penguins 3, Capitals 2	2:19:15	April 24, 1996
6.	Canucks 5, Stars 4	2:18:06	April 11, 2007
7.	Maple Leafs 3, Red Wings 2	2:10:18	March 23, 1943
8.	Stars 2, Sharks 1	2:09:03	May 4, 2008
9.	Canadiens 2, Rangers 1	2:08:52	March 28, 1930
10.	Islanders 3, Capitals 2	2:08:47	April 18, 1987

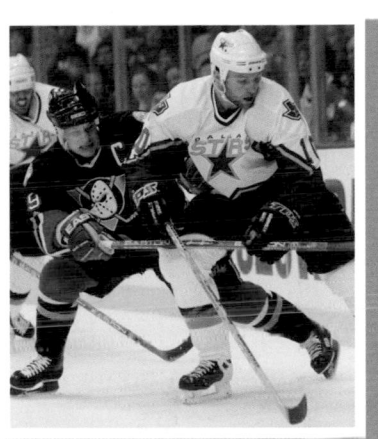
▲ Ducks vs. Stars

RECORD FACT The shortest overtime in playoff history lasted nine seconds. The Montreal Canadiens' Brian Skrudland quickly scored to beat the Calgary Flames on May 18, 1986.

▼ **Claude Provost**

▼ **Claude Provost of the Montreal Canadiens and Denis Savard of the Chicago Blackhawks share the record for the fastest goal to start a period at four seconds.**

▼ **Nels Stewart of the Montreal Maroons and Deron Quint of the Winnipeg Jets each scored a pair of goals just four seconds apart.**

▼ **Bill Mosienko of the Blackhawks scored the fastest hat trick in NHL history. In 1952 he scored three goals in a span of 21 seconds.**

▼ **Jim Dowd**

▼ **The fastest a team has scored two goals is three seconds. The Minnesota Wild pulled off the feat in a 2004 game with goals by Jim Dowd and Richard Park. In 1971 the Boston Bruins scored three goals in a record 20 seconds.**

▼ **The St. Louis Blues and the Boston Bruins each scored a goal two seconds apart in 1987. It took only 15 seconds for the Minnesota North Stars and the New York Rangers to score three goals during a game in 1983.**

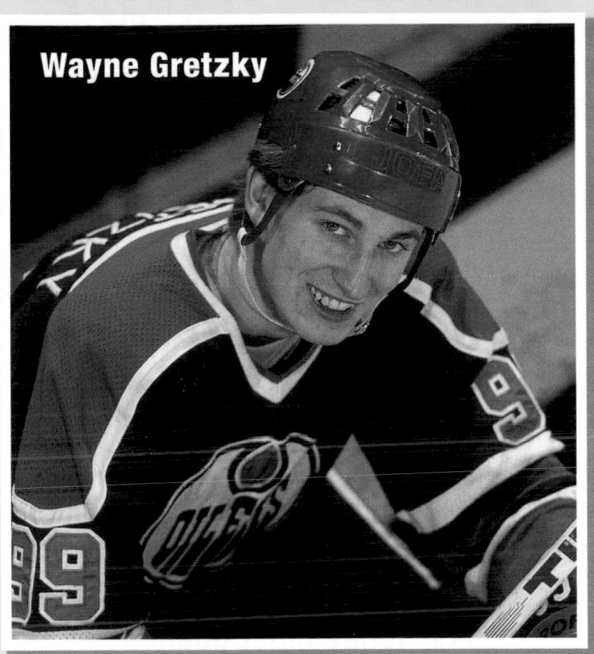

Wayne Gretzky

Jacques Plante

▼ Scoring Streak

Wayne Gretzky started the 1983–84 season with a record 51-game point-scoring streak. The Great One racked up 153 points during the streak. The closest anyone has come to matching it is Mario Lemieux, who scored points in 46 straight games in 1989–90. The longest goal-scoring streak is 16 games set by Punch Broadbent of the Ottawa Senators in 1921–22.

▼ Most Awards

Wayne Gretzky won the Hart Trophy as the NHL's most valuable player a record nine times. The next highest on the list is Gordie Howe, who won the award six times. Bobby Orr won the Norris Trophy as the league's top defenseman eight times. Goaltending great Jacques Plante won the Vezina Trophy as the best goalie seven times.

RECORD FACT Goaltender Tom Barrasso, who played for six teams over 19 seasons, compiled 48 points in his career. Grant Fuhr, who also played goalie for six teams over 19 seasons, had 46 points in his career, including a 14-point season in 1983–84 with the Edmonton Oilers.

TIMELINE

1873	The rules of hockey are first written by James Creighton in Montreal
1877	The first organized hockey team is formed at McGill University in Montreal
1891	The first women's hockey games are played
1893	The first Stanley Cup games are played
1909	The Montreal Canadiens are founded
1917	The National Hockey League is formed; the Seattle Metropolitans of the Pacific Coast Hockey Association become the first American team to win the Stanley Cup
1920	Men's hockey is played in the Olympics for the first time; Canada takes the gold medal in Antwerp, Belgium
1924	The Boston Bruins play in the first NHL game in the United States
1942	The Brooklyn Americans (formerly the New York Americans) fold, leaving the NHL with its Original Six teams
1948	The University of Michigan wins the first NCAA men's hockey championship
1967	The NHL expands to 12 teams
1972	The new professional league called the World Hockey Association is formed; several NHL stars, including Chicago's Bobby Hull, jump to the new league
1978	Wayne Gretzky makes his professional debut with the Indianapolis Racers of the WHA; eight games into the season he was traded to Edmonton
1979	The WHA's remaining teams—the Edmonton Oilers, Quebec Nordiques, Hartford Whalers, and the Winnipeg Jets—merge into the NHL

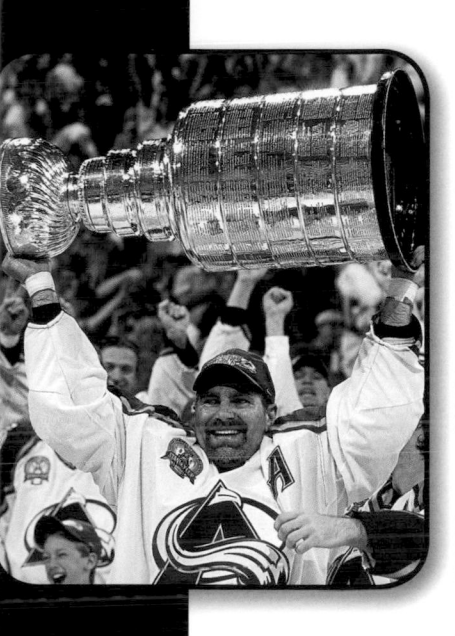

1980	The United States pulls off the "Miracle on Ice" during the Olympics, upsetting the mighty Soviet Union
1998	NHL players compete in the Olympics; women's hockey is played in the Olympics for the first time
1999	Wayne Gretzky retires as the NHL's all-time leading scorer
2004	The NHL season doesn't start because of a disagreement between team owners and players; the season is canceled and, for the first time since 1919, the Stanley Cup was not awarded
2005	Shootouts after overtimes are introduced to regular-season NHL games, meaning there are no more tie games
2010	Sidney Crosby scores the game-winning goal in overtime as Canada defeats the United States 3-2 in the men's gold medal game of the Winter Olympics in Vancouver
2014	The Los Angeles KIngs capture their second Stanley Cup in a three-year span, defeating the New York Rangers 4 games to 1.

Match the current NHL team with its original home.

Carolina Hurricanes	Inglewood, California
Dallas Stars	Landover, Maryland
Arizona Coyotes	Quebec City, Quebec, Canada
Washington Capitals	San Francisco, California
Calgary Flames	Atlanta, Georgia
New Jersey Devils	Winnipeg, Manitoba, Canada
Colorado Avalanche	Boston, Massachusetts
San Jose Sharks	Bloomington, Minnesota
Los Angeles Kings	Kansas City, Missouri

Answer: Hurricanes—Boston; Stars—Bloomington; Coyotes—Winnipeg; Capitals—Landover; Flames—Atlanta; Devils—Kansas City; Avalanche—Quebec City; Sharks—San Francisco; Kings—Inglewood

READ MORE

Frederick, Shane. *The Technology of Hockey.*
North Mankato, Minn.: Capstone Press, 2013.

Frederick Shane et al. *The Ultimate Guide to Pro Hockey Teams 2015.*
North Mankato, Minn: Capstone Press, 2012.

Gitlin, Martin. *The Stanley Cup: All about Pro Hockey's Biggest Event.*
North Mankato, Minn: Capstone Press, 2012.

Morrison, Jessica. *Wayne Gretzky: Greatness on Ice.*
New York: Crabtree Publishing, 2011.

INTERNET SITES

FactHound offers a safe, fun way to find Internet sites related to this book. All of the sites on FactHound have been researched by our staff.

Here's all you do:

Visit *www.facthound.com*

Type in this code: 9781491419625

INDEX